Creating a Preschool Center

*Parent Development
in an Integrated
Neighborhood Project*

Creating a Preschool Center

Parent Development in an Integrated Neighborhood Project

Aline B. Auerbach

*Formerly Director, Parent Development Project,
Bloomingdale Family Program, New York*

*Currently Parent Group Consultant,
Child Development Center of the
Jewish Board of Guardians, New York*

Sandra Roche

*Formerly Administrative Coordinator,
Bloomingdale Family Program, New York*

PHOTOGRAPHS BY NANCY SIRKIS

John Wiley & Sons, Inc.
New York · London · Sydney · Toronto

Preface

This is the story of how a spontaneous neighborhood venture of pre-school playgroups, established by a small group of mothers for their children, grew and grew. Because of the mothers' vision of the only kind of education that they felt could have real meaning in the world today for their children and themselves, the venture became a human relations experiment in which all elements of the local population were included and integrated. Recognizing the importance of the parents in such an educational project, it also became, with support from the Ford Foundation, a demonstration of new approaches by which parents from many backgrounds could learn together for and about their children.

This development took place at a time of great change in the social atmosphere of our large urban centers, when blacks and other minority groups were struggling to find their own place in the larger community. Some felt that their individual dignity and ethnic pride could be fully developed only through *integration* in programs and committees, in which each group would work for and be given the recognition and respect that is its due. Others felt that the same goal could be achieved only by *separating* into two societies—black and white—with blacks taking over the control of black activities in their neighborhoods and lives. This book exemplifies what one small community-within-a-community was able to accomplish, thus far at least, in its struggle to resolve these mounting group tensions and conflicting purposes.

We, the authors, have been involved in this project in different ways and have looked at it from different vantage points. One of us was at first an active participating mother, then a member of the administrative staff and of the board. The other, with long experience in various aspects of the parent education movement, joined the program first as consultant and then as director of the program of parent development.

We feel that this case history is evidence of an important social and educational philosophy—that of relating every aspect of a program to the live experiences and needs of the people it serves. We hope the story of the program's development, procedures, accomplishments, and difficulties will stimulate others to experiment along similar lines. We believe that if our philosophy is sound, each experiment will be different in specific form and detail, but it can demonstrate in many ways the untapped resources that are dormant in all of us.

Moreover, the story is an example of a pragmatic approach in which a deep conviction about human values in a democracy gave rise to an idea of service. In turn, techniques were developed from the ground up, which translated this idea into action. Here social science theory evolved from experience, rather than from having a full blown theory tested by its utilization. Yet the procedures and findings were in keeping with the thinking of such sociologists as Miller and Reissman and others, who have stressed the need to view class and ethnic groups without stereotyping them and to begin deliberately to look at individuals in all "groups" with full appreciation of their positive characteristics.*

Aline B. Auerbach
Sandra Roche

* See S. M. Miller and Frank Reissman, *Social Class and Social Policy*. Basic Books, Inc., 1968.

An Explanation

This book represents the wisdom that came from the parents who gave of themselves so completely to a new and experimental program. They learned a great deal but their struggles and successes can have meaning for the many others who are embarked in programs that recognize the value of true parent participation.

To separate the facts of the Bloomingdale experience itself from what we consider to be its meaning for others, we have indented the sections that suggest some of its implications for general use.

A. B. A.
S. R.

Contents

Creating a Preschool Center

*Parent Development
in an Integrated
Neighborhood Project*

Chapter One
A Program Develops

It's hard to imagine that the Bloomingdale neighborhood really is a neighborhood in the traditional sense of the word—25,000 people packed into a pocket of land between Manhattan's Central Park and the Hudson River—ten blocks that take you from middle-class 96th Street right to the borders of Harlem. The name itself—Bloomingdale—is a legacy from the eighteenth century, when the Bloomingdale farm covered these acres, now in their turn covered completely with concrete, stone, and brick.

This is a neighborhood that has little to hold it together. Middle-income families—largely white, but also black, Puerto Rican, and Oriental—live in rent-controlled apartments along the park or the river. Many of the marriages are interracial. In the center is one of the city's vast public housing

1

projects: Frederick Douglass Houses. In between are many blocks of tenements, tiny overcrowded apartments where black families (many newly arrived from the South), Spanish-speaking Puerto Ricans and Dominicans, and French-speaking Haitians struggle to raise their children. The streets are dangerous. Within this poverty pocket, rates of crime, drug addiction, alcoholism, and tuberculosis are comparable to the East Harlem ghetto across the park.

In one sense, Bloomingdale is a highly fragmented neighborhood. Agencies and committees to organize black parents, Spanish-speaking parents, Haitians, welfare recipients, near-left and far-left groups, tenants, consumers, and drop-outs have proliferated. Each of these groups meets separately, has different (sometimes conflicting) aims, and often struggles against the others for recognition and power.

And yet it is a community. We take a walk across 102nd Street from Central Park to the Hudson River, slicing through a cross section of the area. As we turn the corner at Central Park West we exchange the brick façades and slightly seedy doormen of the avenue for the sights and smells of a slum. Before we reach the next cross street, Manhattan Avenue, we've stopped to chat with three women on a stoop. We ask about each other's children, gossip about the latest public scandal, and make plans to see each other at a community supper the following week. One mother mentions, as she has for the past three years, her plan to move to New Jersey "next month" to get away from the block.

Across Manhattan Avenue the scene changes again. Now we are in Douglass Houses. The concrete walks and tot lots are neat. The lawns are well kept; children are not allowed to play on the grass. Mothers with baby carriages sit on benches and watch their toddlers climb in the standard-issue Housing Authority playground. We overtake the local organizer for the Welfare Recipients' League. We talk about getting parents out to a local School Board meeting. A dozen women call out greetings along the way. Columbus Avenue . . . Amsterdam Avenue . . . Douglass Houses continue. Then Broadway with its shops and supermarkets . . . and its decaying "hotels" where welfare workers house, among the junkies and hookers, families who have been displaced by fires and landlords and who are waiting for relocation. Finally, West End Avenue and Riverside Drive, middle-class and comfortable. Yet all along the route we're met with familiar faces and friendly greetings.

The same scene repeats itself many times every day for hundreds of parents and children who have come to share a sense of community that goes beyond their own class, color, or culture. This spirit has taken root and grown in the Bloomingdale neighborhood despite the thrust of the larger society toward separatism and mutual distrust, and even despite such movements within the neighborhood itself. This sense of community is largely a direct outgrowth of the Bloomingdale Family Program and the people who have been drawn to it during the past decade.

From the very beginning the Bloomingdale Family Program was concerned with the question of community. It was begun in 1960 by Mrs. Juliet Brudney, who had just been named director of the Bloomingdale Conservation Project. (Neighborhood Conservation was a project of the Wagner administration under the leadership of Mrs. Hortense Gabel, the director of City-wide Conservation. It attempted through concerted code enforcement and pressure on landlords to reverse the tide of urban decay in those neighborhoods where much of the housing was still sound.) Mrs. Brudney recognized that neighborhood conservation could not succeed without the involvement of the people who live in the neighborhood. Yet at that time, the neighborhood was as fragmented as its housing patterns.

She recognized, however, that all parents share a natural community of interests where their children are concerned, and so children and their parents became the focus of Bloomingdale's efforts to bring people together. The Bloomingdale office in the Master Institute (a cultural center that included the Riverside Museum and a school of art and music, which had sponsored the Conservation Project since 1959) looked out over Riverside Park where a large playground was virtually unused. Parents had stopped coming there because it was isolated and considered unsafe, and because there was little for their children to do there.

There, in the summer of 1960, the first Family Program took shape. To attract the children (preschoolers as well as older children), an exciting program of creative arts, games, and sports was offered. A staff was "borrowed" from the Park Department, the Board of Education, and the Health Department. The project attracted the attention of two prominent leaders and educators whose chief concern was to improve services for children. Dr. Leona Baumgartner, then Commissioner of Health of New York City, gave it her encouragement and support. Miss Cornelia Goldsmith, at that time Chief of the Division of Day Care and Foster Homes of the New York City Health Department, was also extremely helpful and provided consultation at many points.

A small nucleus of parents, mostly middle-class at the beginning, spread through the neighborhood, publicizing the new program, recruiting children, inviting families, escorting batches of little ones down to the park, widening the circle of people who were learning about this new kind of program—free, for all children, and offering something for parents too.

As word spread, the once-deserted playground became alive with children. And with the children came the mothers. Here, at last, was the chance to bring all kinds of people together around a concern they all shared: their children. Two pioneer parent educators from the Health Department, Billy Clute (now Ginsberg) and Lisa Stein, began to meet with parents informally on the park benches and to enlist their interest, particularly in the program for the preschool children. Most parents, including middle-class parents, were unaware of what constituted a good early childhood program. It was the first time they or their children had ever participated in such a program.

As they watched their children learning to work together, to experiment, to exercise their imaginations and creativity, the parents found themselves participating also. Soon women who had never shared a word or an experience (even though they lived on the same block or in the same buildings) found themselves working side by side as playground assistants or nursery helpers. Others were put to work on fund-raising projects, planning trips or setting up the festival that celebrated the end of the summer program. And from working together, from shared concerns as parents in a city that provided little for its children (whether poor or middle class), a feeling of identity with each other and with the Family Program began to grow.

When that first summer came to a close and the older children prepared to return to school, the mothers realized that the preschool program that had aroused their own and their children's enthusiasm was also going to close. But they could not let it lapse. Having had a taste of what a good preschool program could be, they were willing to work hard and fight for its survival. For this was 1960. Head Start was still five years away, and private nursery school was out of reach even for many middle-class families.

Their resolve to continue the program throughout the year was based also on a deep conviction that children grow and learn best in an environment where they are exposed to all kinds of children. There was a genuine desire on the part of parents to get to know other parents different from themselves, for black and white, living virtually side by side, to begin to do something *together*. And, for many middle-class parents, there was also a commitment to see what could be done for children less fortunate than their own. No matter how patronizing such a view may seem today (and Bloomingdale too has outgrown it, although not without some pain), it represented in 1960 the birth of a social conscience in the Bloomingdale neighborhood, a spirit of caring and concern that has made this a unique community.

RUNNING A PROGRAM WITHOUT FUNDS OR FACILITIES

Bloomingdale's tradition of parent participation grew out of necessity. Without staff or money, the program had only one visible asset—the energies and enthusiasm of the parents who made it work. But even though it grew out of necessity, the intense involvement of parents was the source of positive values that have remained with the program ever since. Thus, in 1960, the parents got together and formed a committee to find a way to keep the preschool program going during the winter months . . . and to keep it a free program. Spearheading this effort was Mrs. Shirley Sarnoff, a parent who remained one of the prime movers of the program for the next seven years.

The Children's Aid Society Community Center at Frederick Douglass Houses donated the use of its large basement space every morning. The Health Department agreed to assign Billy Clute and Lisa Stein to the Family Program on a full-time schedule, so now there was a staff. And the Heckscher Foundation provided materials and equipment.

The Family Program has run year-round ever since, although it has undergone many changes in procedure, location, and range of service. To stay alive, particularly prior to 1965, the program often had to adapt itself to the funds that were available (and the special interests of the funding sources). The only constant elements were the participation in classroom and family room activities required of virtually every parent in the program and the fact that the program was free, integrated, and open to all parents in the community.

Bloomingdale could operate on a shoestring budget only because of the cooperation of city and private agencies. During the summers, the staff members on the city payroll were assigned to the Family Program in a unique arrangement with three different city agencies: the Park Department, the Board of Education (Bureau of Community Education), and the Health Department. Other staff members were hired with funds given by private sponsors such as the West Side Day Nursery and the Master Institute. To these were added volunteers from the neighborhood and from nearby schools and colleges. But although the staff might be drawn from half a dozen different sources, the leadership was Bloomingdale's . . . and they functioned as a team. Often the same workers were assigned to Bloomingdale by the Park Department and the Board of Education year after year, and therefore they became completely identified with the program.

In 1964 Bloomingdale obtained a grant from the Vincent Astor Foundation to experiment with the training and employment of neighborhood teenagers as recreation workers. This was a forerunner of what was eventually to become the Neighborhood Youth Corps. Later, when the antipoverty program went into operation in 1965, the summer staff was strengthened by workers from VISTA, Urban Corps, and Neighborhood Youth Corps, and by staff members hired through Community Action and Head Start grants.

The winter preschool program grew or retrenched according to each year's funding. Gradually the Health Department reduced its involvement with the program as its parent educators began to work with new parent groups starting up in other parts of the city. Funds were lowest in 1963 and 1964, yet the Family Program managed to serve more than 75 children in each of those years by operating playgroups only three mornings a week; the paid staff consisted of two parents, one acting as coordinator and the other as head teacher. All other staff was volunteer, including several parents who taught two or three mornings a week without pay . . . and who kept their commitment for an entire school year, getting babysitters to stay with their own children when sickness or bad weather kept them from school. The program was strengthened by the cooperation of Teachers College, Columbia University, and Yeshiva University, and participation in their special programs or research studies often brought much-needed staff and consultant help.

In 1965 the Institute for Developmental Studies provided funds that made it possible for the Family Program to add a five-day-a-week pre-kindergarten program. Through the Institute, Bloomingdale also took part in teacher-training seminars, and began to work with the new learning materials and techniques they were developing.

The Family Program had, at this point, aroused much interest because of the intense involvement of its families in the program. Thus in 1965 the newly forming Head Start program looked to Bloomingdale as a model for its own program of parent involvement. Many discussions were held with the Head Start central staff prior to the summer of 1965. Bloomingdale sponsored its own Head Start programs during the summers of 1965 and 1966.

As Bloomingdale expanded and broadened its service—through the Institute for Developmental Studies, through Head Start and, as we shall see, through a Ford Foundation grant—it kept its sights focused on its original commitment and goals: an integrated program, representative of the neighborhood, providing a rich learning experience both for young children and their parents.

FORD FOUNDATION GRANT FOR PARENT PROGRAM

That same year, 1965, saw the beginning of a three-year demonstration grant from the Ford Foundation. The demonstration project sought to develop new ways of reaching families from many backgrounds and to help "parents to acquire attitudes and skills that will enable them to understand and meet the developmental and learning needs of small children." It also attempted to give parents relevant experiences that would "lay the foundation for their participation in school and community affairs."*

The Ford grant gave Bloomingdale respite from daily financial crises. Now the energies that had gone into keeping alive could be devoted to program development. The grant also brought problems of its own, which will be discussed later in this chapter, as the parents and the new professional staff sought to find their own roles and responsibilities.

With the Ford grant, the shape of the program for the next three years was stabilized. Between 80 and 100 children were served in each of the three years. The oldest children—the five-year-olds—came five mornings a week. The four- and three-year-olds attended either two or three mornings a week. In each of these groups, a teacher (on the staff) was assisted every day by two parents who "volunteered" their services on a rotating basis. (Volunteering to help, of course, was a prerequisite of admission to the program in most cases.)

Provision was made for the youngest brothers and sisters too. The toddlers had their own playgroup, supervised by mothers. The availability of the toddler group made it possible for mothers with very small children to participate freely in the classroom and to take part in the parent program as well.

There has always been a place for toddlers and infants at Bloomingdale; any program that realistically hopes for the participation of parents must recognize that four- and five-year-olds usually have one- or two-year-old siblings, and that mothers need freedom from the latter before they can lend a hand with the former.

THE FAMILY PROGRAM CHANGES ITS HOME

Shortly after the Ford grant went into effect, Bloomingdale lost its home in the community center and nearly had to close its doors. (The space that the playgroups had used was turned over to a year-round Head Start program jointly sponsored by Bloomingdale and the Children's Aid Society.) From the modern community center the Family Program moved half a block away to a dingy church basement. Despite a new coat of yellow paint inside, it was a dreary place. In the winter the heating system broke down and the church itself was constantly broken into; the play equipment was stolen and vandalized. Yet the parents continued to bring

* From a letter from the Fund for the Advancement of Education (Ford Foundation), stating the purposes of their grant, dated June 7, 1965.

their children and to gather in the church's huge old-fashioned kitchen. Only the five-year-olds continued to meet in the community center.

The following year the program was installed in another church . . . this time a well-kept Presbyterian Church building on 105th Street. Now the program was really spread out, with the five-year-olds two blocks away in the community center, the three- and four-year-old playgroups sharing a giant basement room in the church, while the parents and the two-year-olds were on the fourth and fifth floors. But parents puffed their way up the steep stairs, sometimes with a baby and a toddler tucked under each arm, and participation continued undiminished.

In 1967 the Family Program moved into its present home . . . a large ground floor apartment on 102nd Street just west of Broadway. Here, for the first time, all the older children were together . . . playgroups and prekindergarten. But the parents and toddlers were still separate in a big barren perambulator room in the housing project a block away on Amsterdam Avenue. Eventually all the groups were to be reunited in the new space as the program spread into basement and second floor rooms.

In one sense the annual moves were disruptive and costly. Yet they had a certain value too. Getting out of the Project's Community Center and into the side streets encouraged a kind of integration that might otherwise have been hard to achieve. Many seriously troubled families who were excluded from the housing project felt uncomfortable in the Community Center and often resented those who did live in the project. Yet these were the very families that Bloomingdale most wanted to reach out to. By the time the Family Program moved to its present location, it had moved much closer to its goal of a population representative of the neighborhood, with a steadily increasing proportion of very poor and very troubled families.

THE FAMILIES WHO CAME

Although the Family Program has always been economically and socially integrated, it has been so with varying degrees of success. The lesson Bloomingdale learned was that it's not enough to *want* to run an integrated program; you must know *how* to integrate a program.

For example, setting quotas doesn't guarantee a balanced result at the end. Active recruitment of the very poor is usually necessary, plus supportive services that will enable the family to keep coming. Bloomingdale learned to set realistic and flexible guidelines for the participation of the mothers, understanding that too many demands on an already overburdened parent may drive her away altogether. In some cases mothers were excused from participation and their children were escorted to the program by other parents or by a staff member. Later, many of these same mothers became active participants themselves, as family crises subsided.

Bloomingdale also learned that a realistically integrated program must enroll many more poor families than middle-class families. This makes practical sense. While many mothers—from different social and economic backgrounds—are eager to have their children in a good preschool program, it's much easier for the middle-class mother to get her child to school every day. She has fewer children, fewer emergencies, and more outside help. Her children also have plenty of clothing. If shoes get wet, there's another pair to put on. If it's a cold day there's plenty of warm clothing. The Family Program on a stormy day always has relatively fewer poor children in attendance.

What kind of families took part in the program? Because it required the active participation of at least one parent, the program was not relevant for working mothers. Since it offered only a half-day and (until recently) a split-week program for the children, it could not serve the mothers who needed full day care for their children. The families served, however, represented all economic levels—welfare recipients, low- and middle-income families.

In the early days, because it had to rely largely on parents for fund-raising and staffing, the program encouraged the participation of relatively more middle-class families. With the Ford grant in 1965, however, the program's Board of Directors established as a guideline on intake the ratio of 35 percent middle class to 65 percent poor families. (In view of the composition of the neighborhood, this also meant that most of the middle-class families would be white and most of the poor families would be Negro or Puerto Rican.) This ratio was later modified to include an even larger proportion of poor families.

It seems clear that a successfully integrated program must include a majority of minority-group members if they are to feel free and relaxed about their participation. On the other hand, even a small group of vocal middle-class mothers can present a formidable front.

Of course, describing a group as middle-class, low-income, or welfare recipients actually says very little about them. The experience of Bloomingdale has demonstrated that there is much heterogeneity within each so-called group—differences in background, personality, outlook, and life style. Parents were, in fact, individuals. And they quickly began to look beyond labels and accept each other as the individuals they were.

Bloomingdale has not always been successful in attracting Spanish-speaking families. Strong Spanish-speaking workers on the staff are essential, but are not always easy to find. Enrollment of Spanish-speaking families was highest in 1965 when the director of the program was a Puerto Rican parent worker. Bloomingdale has never had a Spanish-speaking teacher on its staff, although there have been some excellent Spanish-speaking parent workers. Yet the need for Spanish-speaking teachers is particularly acute in the preschool area, since so many of the three- and four-year-olds come to the program speaking and understanding virtually no English at all. We consider the shortage of trained Spanish-speaking teachers as a serious defect of Bloomingdale and many other urban preschool programs and urge foundation and government programs to enable more men and women of Spanish background to obtain professional training to work with preschool children.

HOW FAMILIES WERE RECRUITED FOR THE PROGRAM

The Family Program has become so much a part of the neighborhood that often the parents themselves hardly remember how they first knew about it. In a study of the program, sponsored by Yeshiva University in the spring of 1967,* a sampling of the mothers reported many different sources of information.

The majority of the white families and those with mixed backgrounds first heard about the program through a casual personal contact, the study states. The black and Puerto Rican families often heard about it more formally from a local public school, a Head Start project or community center, as well as by word of mouth from friends and neighbors. Some families first encountered it at a Bloomingdale-sponsored block party or bazaar. "The variety of ways that people heard about the program suggests the extent to which the program is known and the effectiveness of its recruitment procedures," the report concludes.

In retrospect, however, it appears that the recruitment procedures were not always well planned or organized. They were often haphazard and uneven, growing out of random contacts of the staff, parents, and board members. Their common quality was the enthusiasm and almost missionarylike zeal of the recruiters, whose contact with new families took different forms:

1. *Casual Word of Mouth by Parents.* The story of the playgroups and the parents' part in them spread all during the year. This took place natu-

* Phyllis E. Gunther, "Report on the Bloomingdale Family Program," January–June 1967 (unpublished), under the sponsorship of Dr. Vera P. John, Ferkauf Graduate School of Education, Yeshiva University, New York, N.Y.

rally because the program occupied such a big place in the lives of the mothers and their children. Parents were also encouraged to bring their friends to the social events the Family Program staged each year: bazaars, portion suppers, film festivals, cake sales, and family outings.

2. *Community-Wide Summer Programs.* Bloomingdale's large summer programs were its best source of new families. The informal outdoor programs in Riverside Park and later in Central Park provided recreational activities for hundreds of children of all ages and for the mothers as well. Whole families came, often spending the entire day together in the park or on occasional family outings. Other children came without their parents, brought by an older sibling or escorted by a Bloomingdale worker. Many of these families were encouraged to become part of the winter preschool program.

In addition to the park programs, Bloomingdale offered summer Head Start programs in 1965 and 1966. Then, in the summer of 1967, the program was carried to the streets in a project called *The Children's Caravan.* The Caravan was an old school bus that had been transformed into a mobile arts center. Operated under an OEO grant, the Caravan was equipped with books, art materials, records and tapes, and a library of films. Each day the Caravan would pull into a tenement street that had been closed to traffic for the day. The staff—early childhood teacher, parent worker, African drummer, Puerto Rican guitarist, and VISTA Volunteers—would draw the children and adults to the bus for a program of film showings, story hours, games, and art. Hundreds of free books were given to children.

The Caravan went on a regular circuit of selected streets and these blocks welcomed them. While in the first weeks of the program the staff had to deal with hostile men who had appropriated the stoops for dice games and drinking, they soon captured the enthusiasm of the block. At noontime card tables and chairs would be brought down from tiny apartments and mothers would serve lunch to the Caravan crew. At the end of the summer, the staff made sure that all the young children they had come in contact with were placed in preschool programs, whether Day Care or Head Start, public school prekindergarten, or the Bloomingdale Family Program.

3. *Deliberate Recruiting Efforts.* To achieve an economically and racially balanced population, Bloomingdale made special recruitment efforts. At certain times, when the program was being reorganized for a new season or when children were being sought for a new Head Start summer group, there was a concerted effort to reach new families and, particularly, the families that were least aware yet most in need of service. The recruiters—parents and staff—kept their eyes open for small children everywhere and approached their parents at every chance. Parents were ap-

proached on stoops and park benches, in supermarkets and laundromats. On occasion, when they saw children playing together on the street without any adults nearby, or when they observed children who came to the park without their parents, the recruiters followed them home, often trailing behind them up many flights of stairs, to meet their parents and interpret the program to them.

Sometimes children recruited themselves. They watched from windows overlooking the outdoor play area, then pleaded with their parents to bring them, too. Other children who wandered the streets, their housekeys on a string around their necks, would find their way to the church or center that Bloomingdale was using, later to be followed home by a worker. In this way Bloomingdale also uncovered a number of older children who had not been attending school at all.

Little special effort was made to recruit middle-class families. They were always eager to take part in a program that offered a good play experience for their children, and that also gave *them* the opportunity to participate in an integrated community project. At one point, there were so many middle-class families on the waiting list that Bloomingdale brought a group of these mothers together and encouraged them to form their own playgroup, which they did. Another year Bloomingdale ran afternoon playgroups for these families on a tuition-paying basis, thereby helping to defray the cost of the free morning program. Special recruitment efforts were directed toward the families who perhaps least understood the nature and purposes of the program—the more disadvantaged families who until recently were not used to thinking of preschool education for their children, who were often too preoccupied with the burdens of day-by-day living to look for such opportunities, and who were least reached by the usual community resources.

The staff and the actively involved parents recognized that the usual avenues of approach had to be dramatically and aggressively extended if these families were to be reached. To do this, they experimented with . . .

4. *Door-to-Door and "In-Building" Recruitment.* During the early years of the program, Billy Clute and Lisa Stein had set up informal playgroups within tenement buildings to get to know the families better, to understand their needs, and to help them participate by making the larger program more responsive to their needs. Later, "in-building" contacts and approaches were used in recruiting more disadvantaged families for the playgroups as well as for Bloomingdale's summer Head Start programs.

In the tenements and "hotels" housing many families on public assistance, recruiters knocked on doors and rang doorbells. They selected target blocks where they knew there were families with many small children. They encouraged parents from these blocks who were already participating to bring in other families with children. Often one mother would have a coffee hour in her home and invite her neighbors to meet the Bloomingdale staff. Desk clerks and switchboard operators at the hotels were sometimes persuaded to give the names and room numbers of families with small children, who would then be visited by recruiters.

5. *Agency Referrals.* Supplementing recruiting activities at many points were referrals from other neighborhood programs. Referrals came from health agencies in the community, from neighborhood centers and settlement houses, from the public schools through their guidance counselors and parent workers, from Day Care and Head Start centers with long waiting lists for their own services, from welfare recipients and other local action groups, and from housing and relocation offices.

As the program became more widely known, special recruiting efforts became less and less needed. Enrollment of new families seemed to go on its own momentum. Parents continued to bring in their friends and neighbors, especially new neighbors who seemed lost, not knowing where to take their children . . . and themselves.

In all these recruitment efforts, parents and staff members came to know many, many families. Some became interested in the program and were eligible because of their children's ages. But the program was not appropriate for everyone. Some had children who required all day care; others had children with special problems that could not be dealt with in the playgroups, such as marked mental retardation; still others were bogged down with serious situations that took precedence over their small children's educational needs.

It is characteristic of the program that when medical, personal, and social problems became apparent in these recruitment contacts, they were picked up and some action was taken, even when the families did not come into the program for their children. Social work services on the staff were limited and fluctuating but all staff members—teachers, family workers, social work aides, and administrators—accepted without question the responsibility to see that these families received the help they needed. Families were referred to appropriate agencies who were contacted on their behalf for health or psychiatric care, day care, guidance, special welfare grants, family planning, medicare, relocation, and other services.

Families thus served became informal members of the larger Bloomingdale "family." They were urged to join the summer program and were invited to go on Bloomingdale outings or to attend social events held during the year. They were sent notices of various activities and the frequent newsletters. After their immediate situations had improved, a number of them enrolled their young children in the playgroups and thus came into the program officially.

INTAKE WITHOUT PAIN

Once a family became interested in joining the program, the intake was accomplished informally and painlessly. The intake interview was handled by the social worker, a teacher, or a parent worker. Sometimes parents handled intake for each other. Intake information was minimal: vital statistics on names and ages of children, address and occupation of parents. Except where legally required as in a Head Start program, Bloomingdale never asked the income of the parent. After intake, the social worker would ascertain during home visits whether the family was receiving public assistance. This was done so that the staff could better understand the problems confronting the family and be ready to offer appropriate services if necessary. Bloomingdale's reticence in money matters did not come from modesty or shame. Instead, it was a deliberate effort to emphasize the non-institutional character of the program, in contrast to the involved intake of day care, welfare, and many social agencies, and to minimize distinctions between low- and middle-income parents.

ESCORT SERVICE

Bloomingdale found that its work did not end with recruiting and enrolling the families. A big part of the job was helping many of the families to attend and keeping them coming regularly. Teachers and parent workers would usually call or visit the home when a child had been absent for a number of sessions. But there were always some families whose difficulties were so great that they were rarely able to bring their children to the playgroups. It was for these families that Bloomingdale provided escort service. In the early years of the program, the escort would be another parent, one who might naturally pass the escorted child's home on her way to school and who would take responsibility for additional children. Later, when funds allowed, a formal escort service was created, with a special staff person responsible for taking the escorted children to and from school.

The escort worker was far more than a pick-up and delivery service. Often she had to go into the home and help get the children dressed for school. Also, because she saw the mother each day (and the mother seldom got to school herself), the escort worker became an important link between the program and the home. She acted as an auxiliary parent worker whose scene of action was the parent's home. She brought to the parent news of upcoming events and often escorted the family to these social events herself. She kept the mother informed of her children's progress in school. Because the escort worker was able to establish warm neighborly relations with the parents, she was often asked to accompany the teacher or social worker on home visits. (See Chapter Six, "Contacts with Families Outside of School.")

WHY PARENTS CAME

In the study sponsored by Yeshiva University referred to above, the parents were asked why they had joined the program. Quoting from the report:

> "A motivation for all mothers coming to the program was to have their children socialize with other children of the same age. Negro, Puerto Rican and 'mixed' mothers wanted their children to get accustomed to school and the Puerto Rican mothers specifically wanted their children to learn to speak English better before going to regular school.
>
> "The white mothers gave more involved and complex reasons for having chosen this program rather than others that were available to them. They shifted from child-centered reasons to the fact that the program is free, integrated and superior to others in the neighborhood:
>
> > '. . . it is integrated in the real sense. All the mothers get together on the same level . . . it is very good for children not to meet only their type of children.
> >
> > '. . . it brings together people of all kinds. Not only those you meet in the lobby or in your segment of the park.' "

Some parents said they had joined the program because of what it offered for themselves as well as for their children. But the recognition of what they themselves had gained became clear only after they had participated for some time. When they were asked what they would tell new families about the program they stressed what the program offered for parents.

Beyond the generalized feelings of parents as to why they came, they came also for very specific reasons. It filled a real need in their lives. Young mothers are often lonely, particularly when they are newcomers to the neighborhood or the city. Bloomingdale brought them together and helped them to find friends. Bloomingdale was also a place where parents learned new skills in handling and helping their children and where they found they weren't alone in their fears or difficulties. And for the children, of course, it meant freedom from close quarters at home, a place to stretch and grow and test their developing abilities.

Parents came and kept coming because the program was flexible, never rigid. If a mother, temporarily overwhelmed, dropped out for three months, she knew that a place for her child could be found when she returned and that she would be welcomed back without a lecture. A measure of the feeling that parents have for the program is their loyalty to it over many years. Parents send second and third children to the Family Program, even when they can afford other arrangements, and continue to attend social events long after their children have graduated and even after they have moved from the neighborhood.

A PROFESSIONAL STAFF BRINGS A NEW SET OF PROBLEMS

When the parents learned the news that the Ford Foundation (with a supplementary grant from another organization) would supply sufficient funds to provide a professional staff for the playgroups and a parent work staff, everyone was delighted. At last Bloomingdale would be able to offer a coordinated program for children and parents without the pressure of continual fund raising. But the delight soon faded as the new staff came on the scene, a staff that had been hired by the parents to run their program for them. A difficult period of adjustment began, as the parents learned that the professionals they had selected had minds and plans of their own. While the staff often gave lip service to Bloomingdale's special commitment and philosophy, in practice they were subtly changing the focus of the program because of their own special interests.

Two directors in succession, both well-qualified skilled people, found growing parent resistance to their special points of view. One had had some experience in community work but none in early childhood programs. Her overriding interest in theater drew a small group of mothers to an active drama group, but had no appeal to the majority of parents whose concern was to play a more effective part in the development and learning of their children. A second director, expert in preschool programs, had had little contact with parents and was not prepared either to involve them in the program or to develop realistic plans for their participation at their different levels of readiness and interest. Here again parents found the focus of the program shifting away from their own involvement and participation with the teachers and children.

Parents for their part were unwilling to give up powers that they had enjoyed over a long period—powers over intake, purchasing, class makeup, and many other aspects of the administration of a school. At the very time that the public schools were beginning to struggle with the question of how to let parents exercise power within the school system, Bloomingdale had this problem in reverse. How could the parents let the staff function and still keep the program under their own control? The parents began to look back with nostalgia on the noisy informality of the program's early days, and realized that part of the appeal of the program had been its flexible and nonprofessional character.

Ultimately Bloomingdale worked out a staffing plan that seemed to work. First, they recognized that the search for a single director who would have strengths both in working with parents and in early childhood programs was unrealistic. So the search was abandoned, and responsibility for the several aspects of the program was divided among several staff members. The overall planning and direction of the parent program was taken over by Aline B. Auerbach, who until that time had been a consultant to the program. Mary Eccles, who had been its social worker, became coordinator of the daily program with the specific responsibility of involving parents at every level in planning and carrying out the program. And an educational consultant was retained to work with the teachers and strengthen the program for the children.

Second, the parents came to see that if they wanted to preserve Bloomingdale's unique tone, their best source for staff members was their own parent body. While staffing a program with parents has pitfalls too, the positive values far outweighed the drawbacks at Bloomingdale. This policy has continued and even accelerated as the program has produced a growing group of parent alumnae who have gained skills and insights through their experiences and training opportunities at the program that have made them valuable as staff members.* Out of a nineteen-member staff in the Spring of 1970, fourteen were present or former parents of children in the program. These fourteen held jobs ranging from kitchen helper to director of the entire program.

PARENTS AS ADMINISTRATORS AND POLICY-MAKERS

The first year and a half of the three-year demonstration parent program was plagued with difficulties that the parents had never foreseen. Many of these seemed to revolve around the relationships between the parents and the professional staff: a "strong" teacher who dominated and patronized parents, parents who tried to manipulate less experienced teachers, administrators who couldn't work with parents, parents who tried to usurp staff functions. As parents and staff tried to cope with these problems, they began to see where the root of the difficulties lay. Partly, they felt, it was related to Bloomingdale's unique history. Here was a program in which parents had always held the major (and sometimes the only) leadership roles. There were no precedents at Bloomingdale for staff members (and particularly "outsiders") to assume these roles.

---

* "Nonprofessionals learn essentially from doing plus systematic in-service training which can be phased in functionally as needed on the job." S. M. Miller and Frank Reissman, *Social Class and Social Policy* (Basic Books, Inc., 1968).

In a larger sense, however, the struggle between parents and professionals at Bloomingdale has implications for many programs in which parents take part. For the basic difficulty lay in the absence of any clearly defined allocation of responsibilities between parents and professionals. The loosely organized parent governing body that had served the program adequately in its early years had no procedures for dealing with staff effectively. The administrative staff of the program, on the other hand, did not know where their powers began or within what limits they had to operate. The first order of business, therefore, was to revamp the structure of the parent governing body, draw up by-laws under which parents and staff would function, and clarify the entire decision-making process.

A committee of parents began to work on by-laws, and these were formally adopted by the parents in 1968. (See Appendix V.) Following the procedures it set up, a Board of Directors consisting only of parents was elected by the parent body. This Board, which began to function during the final year of the demonstration program, has emerged as a strong executive body, making all policy decisions, being responsible for hiring and firing staff members, and raising and allocating funds. In ethnic and economic terms, the Board became fully representative of the integrated population of the Family Program. Achieving this took work both by the parents and the staff.

> To expect a dynamic contribution from parents who are beset with problems of housing, health, large families and minimal income, is unrealistic unless there is a genuine commitment to making it possible for such families to participate. Meeting times and babysitting arrangements must be set up at their convenience, taking into account, for example, that parents are reluctant today to venture out on city streets to come to meetings at night. Such planning is essential if the decision-making responsibility is to be shared by all groups of parents.

At Bloomingdale, the value of having such a broad decision-making base was put to its severest test in the year that followed the expiration of the Ford grant, as the new Board of Directors was faced with two power struggles that threatened the entire future of the program.

INTERGROUP RELATIONS AT BLOOMINGDALE: SHARING POWER VS. TAKE-OVER ATTEMPTS

It would be misleading to claim that parents in the Bloomingdale program were always one big happy family, with no tensions, that this was an integrated program with no racial overtones. The history of this program parallels a period of intense social change throughout the country and the history of the Family Program reflects these upheavals. In fact, racial animosities often ran high at Bloomingdale. The strength of the program was measured by its ability to withstand such outbreaks of bad feeling—which were often expressed in stormy discussions and angry parent meetings—and to resolve them sufficiently for the program to continue.

In the early years of the program the middle-class (and largely white) parents played a dominant role. They gave their time and energy to the program and worked hard to make it succeed. They also brought to the program a commitment to integration as a way of life for their interracial neighborhood. They had a dream that integration could work in the Family Program and that Bloomingdale could lead the way for the whole community. Therefore, much of their effort went into the task of involving children and parents from the housing project and from the shabby side streets. This process was accelerated during the period of the Ford grant, and black and Puerto Rican parents began to move into roles of responsibility and leadership on the Board of Directors, in parent activities and on the staff. But even though more black faces and Spanish accents could be seen and heard at Board and committee meetings, the tone of these meetings and the direction of the program remained largely middle-class and white.

However, beginning in the closing months of the demonstration project, and throughout the year that followed, Bloomingdale found that its black and Puerto Rican parents were no longer willing to take a back seat and leave the direction of the program to others. A struggle for control of the program began.

On the one hand, with the departure of the Ford-funded staff members, a small group of middle-class parents were clinging to their leadership role. They were caught up in the idea that the Bloomingdale Program was, in a sense, a "cause" to which they were committed. They felt that here they had a chance to better the lot of the poor. Ideologically and intellectually committed to the concept of integration, they still felt they had to take over, to make sure that the project worked. In their eagerness to "do good," they failed to recognize that black and Puerto Rican parents wanted to make their own contribution to the program, *in their own way*.

At the same time, the value of integration was being repudiated by a small group of black parents. The militancy of this group reflected the growing thrust toward separatism that characterized so many movements at this time (1968–1969). These separatist sentiments were no doubt strengthened in reaction to the assertiveness of the middle-class group.

The split in the parent body was also evident in the points of view of the staff. Some staff members were committed to separatism, others to integration, and each group had its influence and following among the parents.

This struggle found expression in the program in many ways. Fund-raising and social events that in the past had brought families closer together, now were occasions for seeming slights and angry feelings. Parent meetings that once were productive of real communication and shared experiences became strained and awkward. Rumors and suspicions ran quickly through the program (often abetted by dissident members of the staff), and fostered an atmosphere of distrust and hostility. Finally, at two large parent meetings, the situation was brought out into the open. Tempers flared, accusations were made, and all kinds of feelings were aired.

The discussions continued in the weeks that followed, and what had begun as a confrontation became a dialogue as the majority of the parents in the program gradually moved closer together. The catalyst for this process was a black parent who felt strongly that integration was meaningful for the children and the parents, and was influential enough to carry other parents with her. In fact, most minority parents *did* like the give and take at Bloomingdale that brought them into contact with many different kinds of families, and they did not want the program to go the way of so many programs in the community which were being organized along rigidly parochial lines—just for welfare recipients, solely for black fathers, or Spanish-speaking adults, for example.

At the same time, the minority parents felt that this was their program too, and they were no longer willing to sit by passively and let a group of aggressive (if well-meaning) middle-class mothers continue to dominate it.

The pulling together of the parent body further helped to strengthen the fledgling Board of Directors, which was now seen as a potentially powerful vehicle for involving the widest group of parents in decision-making.

Faced with this unity of feeling on the part of the great majority of Bloomingdale parents, the power struggle petered out. A few of the more militant black parents simply left the program, as did several middle-class white parents. The large body of parents found themselves working closer together in order to maintain a racially mixed and balanced parent-child group. They now turned their energies to new program possibilities—Head Start and Day Care—that seemed to offer Bloomingdale a more permanent status and less of a hand-to-mouth existence.

Bloomingdale has thus far been able to reconcile divergent groups within its program by building on the commonality of aims and problems shared by *all* parents in relation to their children and their community. In so doing, however, it must be recognized that Blooming-dale has not been able to accommodate extremes of opinion. Since it is self-selective, it attracts primarily those who are in sympathy with its goals. Those who are not eventually drop out. The group that remains, while it can tolerate a fairly wide spectrum of opinion, shares a basic commitment to the value of integration in a com-munity. But neither Bloomingdale nor the host of community or-ganizations serving special interest groups has succeeded in com-pletely bridging the gulf that separates the many groups that make up a racially and economically mixed neighborhood.

NEW DEVELOPMENTS FOLLOWING THE COMPLETION OF THE DEMONSTRATION PROJECT

Despite the fact that its major source of funds was cut off after the com-pletion of the Ford Foundation grant, the Family Program managed not only to survive but actually to increase the number of children served in the program. Two new developments in the program made this possible.

First, part of the burden of staff costs was assumed by the VISTA pro-gram. Traditionally, VISTA had selected outside volunteers with some University training or job skills and sent them into poverty areas to work with local groups. Now for the first time, VISTA was persuaded to recog-nize as equally valid the early childhood training that parents had received as participants in the Bloomingdale program. Accordingly, several Bloom-ingdale parents were accepted into the VISTA program and, paid by VISTA, were reassigned back to their own community—to the Blooming-dale program where they became the nucleus of the teaching staff under the direction of a head teacher. At Bloomingdale, the practice of training and employing parents to work in the classroom long predated the present movement to hire paraprofessional workers in the public schools and other community institutions, and parents had always served in all kinds of staff capacities. Now, with the help of VISTA and on-going in-service training, Bloomingdale was able to employ parents to fill almost every staff role.

A second development that enabled Bloomingdale to weather the loss of funds was the decision to ask the parents who could afford it to pay a modest tuition fee. Out of some 100 children who attended the program in 1968–1969, about half were tuition-paying. The fees, however, were modest indeed ($5 or $10 a month), and each parent made her own deci-sion as to what, if anything, she could comfortably afford. Also, for the first time, the program operated full groups in the afternoons as well as the mornings, thereby increasing the number of families who could be served and making more efficient use of its classroom facilities.

By the close of the first year on their own, the parents could point with pride to a school year successfully completed, a parent body that was newly reorganized and strengthened, and, even more important, a future that was made more secure as negotiations with Head Start and Day Care moved toward fruition. In July 1969, the Family Program began operation as a year-round Head Start Center. Its belief in integration was not lost in the process, for together with the Head Start program Bloomingdale is maintaining a parallel program of tuition-paying children, most of whom are white. The Head Start children (in themselves an integrated group) and the smaller number of parallel program children participate jointly in the program as do the parents.* Furthermore, despite the fact that nearly a third of the parents are working parents, parent participation is still very much a way of life for Bloomingdale. Those who cannot assist in the classroom or join in Family Room activities during the day, participate in other ways, making handcrafts for a bazaar or helping to run a portion supper. Directing the entire program with creative imagination and endless energy is Mrs. Susan Feingold, one of the founding mothers of the Bloomingdale Family Program.

Another project being developed is the conversion of Bloomingdale's former office and barnlike perambulator room in the housing project into a day care center, to provide yet another extension of the Family Program into an area of great community need. An architect-parent has already completed the designs for the renovation of the space, costs for which are to be borne by the Division of Day Care. This project would also be enriched educationally through the close cooperation of the Bank Street College of Education. The Day Care Center would present a special challenge to the Family Program to develop a program for parents who are away at work during normal school hours. Bloomingdale is eager to tackle this challenge.

In the meantime, Bloomingdale continues to sponsor, in addition to the Head Start and parallel program, a toddler program for younger siblings of Head Start and parallel children, an after-school tutorial center (manned by Columbia University students) for older siblings of the Head Start children, and the perennial summer program in Central Park. This is a community helping itself, accomplishing large objectives by pooling the talents and energies of a great many "ordinary" people. Other communities can do the same, and the following chapters outlining some of the ways the Family Program has found helpful in developing parent abilities, may point the way for other programs.

---

* The parallel program families, although ineligible for Head Start under its current economic guidelines, still fall largely into the low income group and pay minimal fees on a sliding scale.

Chapter Two
Parents Come to School

Parents, too, come to school in the Bloomingdale Family Program. They come to help the project run smoothly but they also come to learn, although they aren't always aware of this. The group of mothers who had started the program, however, knew what it had meant to them, personally, as well as to their children. And so they had asked for—and received—the grant from the Ford Foundation to develop an experimental, coordinated program of parent education and development that would open up to all the parents the opportunity to learn more about children and incidentally about themselves.

There were few guidelines for such a comprehensive parent program.

There was, of course, the long but uneven history of cooperative nursery schools. In the broad field of parent education many different kinds of educational programs had been developed in a variety of settings.* Many were sporadic and isolated. Few really attracted parents from all segments of the community. They did, however, offer a body of experience from which one could draw selectively for new purposes.

This the Bloomingdale Program attempted to do, with much experimenting, considerable success, and some disappointments. The parents themselves showed the way, as they began to assist the teachers in the classrooms, joined in activities in the Family Room, served on various committees and on the board, and became involved in every part of the project. So, in practice, they found their places, some participating more in one activity, some in another. And the statement of their responsibilities—and opportunities—which had been given them in a Handbook when they registered their children, began to have real meaning.†

But their first real contact with the program came when they entered the classrooms with their children. Here they were all expected to take their part.

PARENTS' FIRST DAYS IN THE CLASSROOM

For a new parent, the first day in the classroom with the children—including her own—was a confusing one. If she came on the first day of a new season, there were many new parents who were as bewildered as she and there was consolation in numbers. Following the practice of many preschool centers, parents were asked to stay until their children made the transition from home to preschool and were able to be left to function comfortably on their own. Here, however, parents were required to help in the classrooms, and it took time for them to know what this meant. It also took time for the teachers to work out an orderly plan so that some mothers could help where they were needed, while others sat quietly on the side, available if their children wanted to come to them for reassurance. In the meantime, the parents all stood around watching their own children out of the corners of their eyes and, of course, comparing them with the other children in the room. If a child entered late in the school year, he and his mother were apt to stick out like sore thumbs. In any case, the teachers and parents who had been in the program before helped new parents to find their places and to learn what to do.

---

* See Aline B. Auerbach, *Trends and Techniques in Parent Education: A Critical Review.* Child Study Association of America, 1961; and *Parents Learn Through Discussion: Principles and Practices of Parent Group Education.* John Wiley and Sons, 1968. Also see Orville G. Brim, *Education for Child-Rearing.* The Free Press, 1965 (paperback).
† See "The Parents' Handbook," Appendix I.

In the first year of the parent program, before plans were developed in an orderly fashion, not even the teachers knew just what the parents were to do, or on what basis. On many days parents cluttered the playrooms, sitting around the edges like birds on a fence, feeling they had to be there, but not knowing how to act. At first they merely sat and watched, not even talking to one another. After the novelty wore off, they began to chatter to one another, adding to the atmosphere of confusion in the rooms that were so crowded with *bodies* that the children and teachers could hardly find their way to the play equipment! On other days, parents vanished after bringing their children, despite the rules, so that there were few if any adult hands, even in the Family Room, to help if they were needed.

At this point, on the recommendation of the parent consultant who later became the director of the parent program, a number of changes were instituted to add structure to the experiment. Simple procedures were set up to insure that two parents would be on hand in each classroom every morning on a rotating schedule, and in staff meetings, staff seminars, and parent class meetings, efforts were made constantly to clarify for parents and teachers just what was expected of parents as teacher assistants.

And so gradually order came into the playrooms and much of the earlier tension was eased for the children, the parents, and the staff.

But even when they began to help with the children as the teachers asked them to do, parents did so in their own characteristic ways.

Mrs. K., for example, tried hard to keep her very active twin boys off the large climbing apparatus in the "gym" area because they became too excited by the physical freedom and, she thought, got too rowdy and made too much noise. She kept saying they should be quiet and *behave*. Only after some weeks did she come to accept the idea that here shouting and running around were all right and that the equipment was there just so children would have a chance to use their bodies in vigorous play and let off steam.

Mrs. T. took her turn in the toddler room and barked orders like a drill sergeant. She did so, however, with warmth and a smile and the little ones fell in line because it was fun.

Mrs. I. barked orders at the children, too, but without love and humor, more in terms of wanting to get things done. She would also shove her own child away each time he wanted to come to her, which only made him want to cling to her the more.

Mrs. N. held her child on her lap endlessly—literally for months—and couldn't see beyond him to the other children. Only when she was able to let him go on his own was she able to be of any help. The teacher soon saw the situation and for a long time didn't count on Mrs. N. to assist; she kept her eye on Mrs. N., however, and encouraged her to let the boy experiment bit by bit in his play with the other children until one day he—and his mother—were both able to take the big step.

Mrs. G. always felt that she had to be "teaching" something to some child every minute. She saw in time that there were many things children learned through play without being "taught." She began to use a gentler kind of suggestion and consciously introduced new words to enrich the children's vocabulary in relation to what they were doing, without making a big "do" about it.

Mrs. D. always busied herself with cleaning chores, which were a great help, and hesitated to become directly involved with the children. She kept her ears open to what the teacher was doing, however, and ultimately became a fine teacher assistant as she became more sure of herself.

Mrs. J. found any excuse for staying out of the classroom altogether because she felt so inept. She changed almost not at all because she didn't give herself a chance.

But many others picked up quickly from the teachers and the other parents, learning, like the children, without being "taught."

The brief stories of these mothers suggest some of the rough spots that have to be ironed out as mothers take part in the classrooms. They show that some parents are better able than others to help children in their play activities. And they have strong preferences, too. At Bloomingdale, some enjoyed making it easy for children to paint or use play dough; others found this much too messy. Some felt more comfortable reading stories or helping with games that had some obvious implications for "learning." Others were too shy to try at first but later found they had real talent in such things as singing games. One mother, for example, who participated slowly in the beginning, seemed to find herself in the classroom and later, in her third year in the project, became an assistant teacher on salary through the VISTA program.

These variations seemed to be determined largely by the personality, make-up, and previous experience of the individual parents. Some more general patterns emerged in the Bloomingdale experience, however, that seemed to be characteristic of different cultural and ethnic groups in the program, and that influenced the mothers' performance in the classrooms.

The teachers reported, for example, that many black and Puerto Rican mothers were continually anxious to have their children behave well, and when *they* were there kept admonishing them. Some, like Mrs. K., tended to find the classroom atmosphere too free, feeling there should be more structure, more discipline, less noise and were inclined to put a damper on the children's spontaneous high spirits. Others made a big point of cleanliness ("don't get your hands so dirty") and proper (too proper) clothes. At first several mothers on public assistance sent their children to school dressed as if they were going to a party, whereas middle-class children appeared in casual overalls and playclothes. A number of Puerto Rican mothers, like Mrs. N., tended to be protective of their own children and watched them closely, giving less attention to the others in the group.

As for the white mothers, many of whom had had more extended education, the teachers felt that on occasion some were inclined to be bossy and often told the other mothers what to do. Inevitably this caused undercurrents of resentment from the other parents and some discomfort in the dictatorial parents themselves, who often said they didn't like the role they were playing. At the same time, many white parents came into the classroom urgently wanting to help *all* the children. In doing so, they sometimes went overboard, like Mrs. I., in *not* responding to their own children until the others were taken care of.

It seemed that all families from whatever background came to the playgroups desperately eager to have their children learn and especially eager for them to learn to read early. They put considerable pressure on the teachers to let them do more about this in the classrooms and at home, although they were not sure just how to go about it. The matter of reading came up again and again—in the Family Room, in the class group meetings and in individual parent-teacher conferences. And why wouldn't parents be concerned, with the emphasis that is currently being put on children's reading, and the wide publicity that is being given to the failure of the public schools to teach reading adequately? For many black and Puerto Rican families, reading has become a symbol, a key to future success in the world, almost a guarantee that their children will accomplish what they may not have been able to do themselves. For many white families, it represents an important first step up the academic ladder. To meet the parents' feeling of urgency, the teachers had to interpret again and again that they were constantly but indirectly preparing children to learn to read, in almost everything they did. At every point, they attempted to stress the many ways in which the school was expanding the children's experiences toward this end. The children were learning to identify and distinguish colors, for example, and the shapes and size of objects, using their small muscles in the simple task of writing their names, constantly learning the words for things around them and for ideas that are part of our daily lives, such as time, space and even human feelings and relationships. All these activities and more, the teachers kept saying, slowly provide a wide base for the children's ability to transfer the *spoken* word to the forms they begin to identify as the *printed* word.

This point of view was reinforced on one occasion in an evening meeting conducted by an early childhood education specialist. Many parents, fathers as well as mothers, came that night and seemed—temporarily, at least—to lose some of their sense of pressure about reading and to accept somewhat more peacefully the long-term educational value of a rich play experience for children.

WHY HAVE MOTHERS IN THE CLASSROOM AT ALL?

There were three good reasons for mothers being in the classrooms. The first was expediency. With only a small teaching staff, the mothers' help was essential in keeping the classrooms operating smoothly for the children.

A second reason was the regulations under which the program operated. Special Health Department rulings stipulated that, as the program was then set up, the mothers, and not the teachers, were responsible for the safety and well-being of the children in the two- and three-day-a-week play-groups. These groups were in the charge of carefully selected, experienced teachers who, however, were not fully licensed. The mothers were expected, therefore, to be either in the classrooms or in the Family Room where they could be on call if they were needed. (For three years the program also included a five-day group, with a licensed teacher; while these parents did not have to take official responsibility for the children, they were still expected to help in the classrooms.)

Third, participating in the classrooms as teacher assistants was the logical first step in the parents' learning more about children and how they grow and develop. This became the core of the larger educational program. It was in the classroom that ideas about children were sparked. From there these ideas fed into class group meetings, group discussions in the Family Room and, ultimately, into the community.

But the parents realized this at first only in bits and pieces. And they were so busy doing the day-by-day school chores and joining in special projects as they came up that they had little chance to think about the meaning of the whole experience. Many of the parents only understood this later, sometimes only when their children had gone into other school settings. Then they looked back with nostalgia to the excitement and satisfactions the Bloomingdale program had brought not only to the children but to themselves.

HOW TO EASE THE MOTHERS' FIRST DAYS:
SUGGESTED TECHNIQUES

In looking back on the experience of Bloomingdale parents in the classrooms, it is clear that much more could have been done to make explicit the part the parents can play as teacher assistants. It is not enough for the teachers to provide the model for parents to follow in guiding and "teaching" the children. They need to put in words not only *what* teachers and teacher aides should do but *why* they do it. Obviously this cannot be accomplished all at once. It must be begun at the start of the season, and continued directly and indirectly as the year progresses. The following procedures may be helpful:

A meeting should be held of the parents of each group within the first few days of school at which each teacher explains very simply the rotating schedule for parent participation in the classroom, outlines the role of the teacher assistant as a true aide to the teacher, and describes the general program plan of children's activities. In practice, the part played by the aide cannot be spelled out specifically in advance: it has to be flexible, depending on where she is most needed, as the children group and regroup in their different play areas and as they interact smoothly or not so smoothly. At one time she may have to be a stimulator of activity, bringing out some kind of play material to challenge the children, such as picture lotto or paper and paint; at another she may be a gentle policeman, seeing that each child has his turn; or she may suddenly have to be a diverter, when she sees trouble brewing between two belligerents. She will be called on to meet many unpredictable situations. But always she takes her cue from the teacher, who sees the program as a whole and indicates to her aides—sometimes in words, sometimes with a gesture—where she sees the need for them to step in. It is essential, however, that the aides too begin to see the program as a purposeful whole so they know that they are doing more than busy-work or just keeping the children occupied.

Since all the parents participate in the classroom at some time, the "message" of what they can do is reinforced and reclarified in regular meetings of the parents of each playgroup with their teacher. These meetings should be held at least once a month, and preferably more often. Here, the different activities should be discussed in terms of their contribution to the children's development. Since the purposes of these activities vary, it is best to explore them one at a time.

Based on their observation of children at play, parents can be helped to see how different activities foster many aspects of the children's growing powers—large physical development and the smaller manipulative ability they will later use in writing, understanding variations in the forms and size of objects they will use in learning to read, identifying objects in words that lead to language development, the use of all materials for problem solving and for the infinite variety of imaginative play through which children work out their fantasies and experiment with testing their ideas against reality.

This kind of understanding comes slowly but it builds up so that the parents come to realize that the different activities are part of a planned "curriculum," whose purpose is to give children a chance to develop many aspects of their abilities and personality.

When the parents begin to find the activities they feel most comfortable with, they should be assigned wherever possible to help in these areas during free play periods—perhaps the doll corner, the play kitchen, story telling, block-building, easel or finger-painting, play dough, or whatever. The assignments should rotate, however, so parents can learn how to help children in different activities. And again they should see themselves as *helping* the children, encouraging them to use materials in their own way, at their own speed, giving a hand when they are really stuck with a problem, but not dominating them.

Wherever possible, parents find it easier to work with the children if simple, written guidelines are posted for each activity. At the easels, for example, a sign might read: "Be sure children put on their aprons before they begin to paint. Put out only a few primary color paints in the jelly glasses for the younger children to use. They will soon learn to mix their own colors. See that the glasses for paints are about half full; this will give the children enough paint for their brushes, but not so much that it will spill over. When a child has said he has finished his picture, don't ask him what he has made. (He often doesn't know himself.) But put his name on it, tear the paper off and leave a fresh sheet for him to use if he wants to. After painting is over, be sure the brushes are washed clean and put away; often the children like to help with this."

Similar instructions at the blocks, in the book corner or at the play-sink and stove should give practical instruction about handling materials along with suggestions as to their use, so that the parents can encourage the children to develop for themselves the capacities each activity can stimulate.

On occasion, the teacher may call on a parent-aide to concentrate on one child, sitting with him at a table, perhaps, as he is working on a simple picture puzzle or reading him a special story, sometimes taking him on her lap if he seems upset or in need of comfort. Parents are often pleased to see that giving a child a brief respite from the group or having him know that he is getting full attention from a grown-up can often help him over a bad or restless time and give him some special reserve strength he can draw on when he goes back into the group. If a mother's own child is in the room while this goes on, she may find her little one at her side wanting some of this special care, too. If this happens, there is always room for two, at least for a while, and her own child may leave soon of his own accord if he isn't rebuffed.

EFFECT OF THE MOTHERS' PRESENCE ON THE CHILDREN: GOOD OR BAD?

Now that more and more mothers are taking part in preschool programs throughout the country, it is important to watch the ways in which a mother's presence may help or even hold back her child's development. On this point, Bloomingdale mothers have had some definite ideas.

On the plus side, they felt that it helps children to make the first big step away from home if their mothers are there with them. Even if they aren't in the room all the time or even every day, somehow the idea seems to get across to children that just because mommies are in and out, home and school are really not two different worlds. The mothers serve as a connecting link between the two and their presence is reassuring and supportive.

On the other hand, many parents felt their being in the room or even nearby in the Family Room made it more difficult for their children to separate from them. It is understandable that they turn to their mothers rather than the teachers when they are in trouble and, of course, the parents can't just push them away. It seems to take these children longer to realize that they can get help from teachers and other mothers just as well. But, in time, the children all seem to learn that other grownups can take over, too, whether they talk in just the same way or not. All together, they merge into a helping figure whom they can trust.

Clearly, whether a child separates easily depends on his experience up to this point—and on his parents' attitudes and understanding. Here, for example, some of the parents had to push their children into being "independent" at home because of necessity, and even four-year-olds often had to take care of themselves to an amazing degree. When it came to taking part in the playgroup, however, they seemed to cling to their mothers just as many of the others did. It was as if the independence that had been forced on them was more than they were ready for. Their psychological development had not gone far enough for them to incorporate the behavior that had been demanded of them into their personality structure in a sound way. Beneath their pseudomaturity they were often babies still. And the new, strange situation often threw them back to expressing an earlier need that had not been fully met.

And what about the mothers? They all wanted their children to be independent, but they went about it in different ways. Many black mothers and white mothers wanted their children to stand on their own feet so badly that they literally pushed them into the classroom on the first day of school and then disappeared, thinking this would *force* their youngsters to be independent. (And this, despite the directive given at registration, that here, as in other preschool programs, parents were expected to stay with the children the first day or two—or more—until they felt "at home" in the school setting.) In contrast, other mothers, particularly some of the Puerto Rican ones, were uncertain about their children's ability to manage without them and were protective of them, even to the point of seeming to be overprotective. Sometimes they admitted that they liked the children to be near them—and did not want them to grow up too fast.

Undoubtedly they had good reasons—personal and also cultural—for wanting to "protect" their children in what may appear to many of them as a strange and even hostile environment. Unfortunately, many schools as well as the urban community as a whole offer little reassurance that individual children will be adequately recognized and looked after, especially those who come from other cultures. No wonder, then, that these mothers often encourage their children to stay close to them until they are certain they can look after themselves. For these children, the period of separation is understandably prolonged.

Some of these attitudes were worked out and modified to a degree as the mothers talked together in their class groups, compared their children's problems in separating with problems of other children, and began to look more realistically at what to expect of their own children. And their anxieties relaxed as they watched the other mothers in the classrooms and gained confidence in their good will and competence in relating to *all* the children as well as their own.

For the children, the hardest part of having their mothers as teacher assistants was having to share them with the other children. This was true whether their mothers were in their own room or an adjoining one. This problem was accentuated in the toddler room where the mother was not just an assistant, but was in charge as the teacher. One toddler-mother-teacher found that it was not possible for story hour and circle time to take place unless her own two-year-old was comfortably sheltered in her lap. Some of the older children took it hard, too. It looked almost as if having to share their mothers with other children in school was just a repetition of what went on in these families at home. If a child was caught up in a strong rivalry situation, it only made it worse to have the situation reenacted in the playgroup; if he had already made some peace with the problem, he seemed better able to throw it off at school. Yet, somehow, they all seemed to learn in their own way that even if they had to wait, in the long run they got taken care of.

It was primarily the mothers who participated in the classrooms. But sometimes a father came regularly when his wife worked in the daytime and he worked at night. They were a great asset, taking over the workbench and helping the children with their hammers and nails and supervising their outdoor play. Having them there was a special treat for children from fatherless homes; the men often became the center of small groups of children who followed them everywhere.

Fathers are often hesitant to appear in the classrooms. Some of them seem to feel this is "women's work" and that they don't really belong. If their schedules permit, however, they often respond when they are asked to come, sometimes shyly at first, then with great interest as they see the children responding to them.

It is well worth making a concerted effort to include fathers. Invite them to come to visit on work holidays when the center is open, as a first step. Before you know it you may have regular helpers.

PARENT-TEACHER GROUP MEETINGS

During the period of the Ford Foundation funding, each teacher met with the parents of her group in regular meetings at the end of the morning, sometimes once a month, sometimes twice a month. The sessions lasted anywhere from twenty to forty-five minutes. Brief though they were, they were important in the educational plan. First, in these sessions the parents brought out their questions about what they had seen in the classroom. Why, they sometimes asked, did the teacher introduce a new activity, like using the "gym" equipment, when the children seemed contented with what they were doing? Or why didn't she step in when Sally and Deborah were brewing for a fight over who should have a favorite puzzle? Or is it okay to have Tommy play in the doll corner so much; isn't that for girls? And what about little Sue who paints the same scrambled picture day after day; shouldn't she be encouraged to try something different? And more.

And they asked about whether they had done the right thing as teacher assistants. Did they take the proper cues from the teacher? Should they have done more themselves with the children? Was it good—or not—that they spent so much time with one child, like Dolores, who seemed to be more content when a grownup was sitting next to her? Or were they doing too much *for* the children rather than *with* them?

The talk back and forth usually began with specific situations and how to meet them, yet what came out was not only a better grasp of what the children's activities are all about but also a better sense of the mothers' own part as teacher assistant. In the discussions, they often said how difficult they found their double role: as parents of their own children and as objective observers and assistants dealing with other people's children. They said they felt pulled between the two. And, on occasion, they also mentioned that it was a ticklish business to talk about an individual child in these sessions, particularly if his parent was present. While in one sense these meetings were like staff meetings of teachers with their assistants, at times they also had the emotional overtones of a group of parents concerned about their children. And they often shifted from one to the other. At first the teachers were scarcely aware of these transitions. When it was brought to their attention in seminar,* they became more sensitive to the double focus and tried to keep the two distinct where possible. The reactions of the parents as teacher assistants belonged in the parent-teacher class meetings; it was suggested that they bring their questions and concerns as parents to the parent discussion meetings† in the Family Room.

But perhaps the most important value of these group sessions was that they served as a kind of safety valve, a place where the parents could bring out their annoyances and dissatisfactions. And speak out they did! They even criticized one another, although they usually did so quite gently. Why didn't Mrs. G., for example, help in cleaning up at the end of the morning? And why did Mrs. B. always hog reading aloud to the children, when others wanted to do this, too? And they aired more serious grievances at times. On one occasion, two Puerto Rican mothers said flatly that the white mothers were not giving enough attention to the Spanish-speaking children. That was why they were there so often themselves, they said, in order to be sure that their children weren't being overlooked. This complaint came as a complete surprise to the teacher and the other mothers. They thought it had no basis in fact—and said so—but the discussion alerted them to be watchful in the future to be *sure* that they responded to each child in terms of his own needs.

But the parents' most recurrent gripe was that some of the mothers were asked to assist in the classrooms more than others, in spite of the rotating plan. Inevitably, in each group there were one or two mothers who were especially helpful; the teachers naturally turned to them when, for one reason or another, parents found they weren't able to live up to the schedule. Even though mothers are flattered to be asked to give extra help, they can get quite irritated if they are called on to do much more than their share. It is hard for them to realize that some mothers have heavier de-

* See Chapter Five.
† See Chapters Three and Four.

mands on their time—and perhaps more immediate problems—than they do. Talking it out in the class groups gave them some better understanding of the hardships many families are struggling with, but it didn't do away with their strong feeling that they were being imposed on.

The whole question of escorted children is one that was never successfully resolved in the Bloomingdale Program. The service was offered to families who needed it, as a way of reaching into the community and bringing in children who could benefit from being in a controlled setting with other children, away from home. Yet there was a basic contradiction here. On the one hand, this was a program in which parents participated and were expected to participate; on the other, children were accepted whose parents could not participate. Although the prime motive had some justification—to serve children most in need of the program—the participating parents tended to regard the parents of the escorted children more as clients than as fellow participants.

Yet every time the Board discussed eliminating the escorted group, they thought of those parents whose children were escorted for a year or two and who ultimately became full-fledged participants and fast friends. Then they decided that the escort service was worth the trouble, as long as it was accompanied by a real attempt to stay in touch with the parents and bring them into the Bloomingdale orbit whenever possible.

These, then, were some of the matters that were brought up in class meetings by the parents. It was the teachers, of course, who conducted these sessions and they had a delicate role to play here. They, like most early childhood teachers, were, by and large, not prepared to work with parents, especially in groups. In the plan of the Bloomingdale parent program, however, the teachers were seen as an important link in the total educational scheme. Accordingly, provision was made to give them special help in staff seminars, so they could comfortably move into what was, for them, a new field of operations. (See Chapter Five.)

Chapter Three
Parents in the Family Room

The term "Family Room" has a pleasant, homelike connotation and set the tone for what went on there. In the Bloomingdale Program, the term became a distinct entity in itself, carrying with it a plan and a purpose through many changes in its location. The first year of the parent program, the Family Room was the large, clumsy, old-fashioned kitchen in the dilapidated church. In cold weather, the hot water pipes banged when the heat was on, and the parents huddled together in their coats around an oilcloth-topped table when the heat was not on. The second year, it was a small room on the fourth floor of the more modern church building, with no water except in an adjoining lavatory and very little space to move around in. The third year it was a part of a large barracklike room in a housing project annex, ordinarily used for storage, again without a sink. And after the parent program ended officially as a Ford Foundation-sponsored demonstration, it was a (smallest of all) room with one window in the apartment quarters used by the playgroups. Here ten people seemed like a crowd, and yet when parent discussion meetings led by the former parent program director drew as many as twenty people, there still seemed to be room. Regardless of the surroundings, the programs of the Family Room continued—but, certainly, with some ups and downs—and they served many different purposes.

The coffee urn moved as the Family Room moved, and continued to be the center for the friendly, social exchange that was the basis for all that went on. Here parents came when they were not assisting the teachers—to relax, to talk, to make things needed in the playgroups, to sew for themselves if they wanted to and, again and always, to talk. Sometimes the mothers brought their infants, in their arms, in baskets or strollers or carriages. Often their just-beginning-to-walk little ones staggered around the edge of the table where the mothers sat. Or their toddlers came in and out from the special alcove or adjoining room the program had set up for them. They came in looking to their mothers for reassurance and then went off again to play on their own. Usually the toddlers were supervised by one or two of their mothers. Most of the toddlers were siblings of children in the program who, of course, could not be left at home. Others, however, were young children of families who had been in the program before and were eager to have their little ones learn to be with other children their own age. The mothers in the Family Room kept their ears open for the first peep of trouble, not only from their own children but from others whose mothers might be busy at the moment. Quickly they moved in and the problem was generally settled without any fuss.

The Family Room was also the place for a variety of activities, planned by the parents. Here they organized several kinds of activities for themselves—a sewing class, a dance group, a drama group, an English class for Spanish-speaking mothers, a Spanish class for English-speaking mothers. This was before self-development projects such as these came to be widely offered under various governmental auspices. Although they were initiated with some enthusiasm from the parents, in time they all seemed to peter out, possibly because of inadequate leadership. Also it may have been that the parents sensed that they were there primarily because of their children and what would benefit *them*.

And so they turned to other activities. They held all kinds of committee meetings (see Parents' Handbook, Appendix I, p. 6), planned fund-raising activities, made things for the annual bazaars, arranged for family outings on weekends or holidays or, if they chose, took part in scheduled meetings of different kinds. These included informal discussion groups meeting regularly on matters of continuing concern to parents at home, in school, and in the community and larger meetings on special topics that were timely and urgent. Here, too, they prepared the frequent newsletters that kept all Bloomingdale families up to date on current happenings. (See sample newsletters, Appendix IV.)

The Yeshiva study gave this report of the Family Room:

"The parents generated a friendly, accepting and comfortable atmosphere, although certain parents dominated the conversation at times. Parents of the same ethnic and socio-economic group tended to gravitate to each other unless a special formal activity was scheduled.* Friendships seemed to develop among parents across ethnic lines in some cases, but less so across socio-economic lines, according to parent comments and observations by staff.

"There was a considerable amount of give and take without regard to ethnic and racial background, even with the sensitive topic of how to handle the question of race with the children. One white mother . . . felt that all mothers had, in addition, joined together to understand and help non-English speaking mothers, whose attendance was just fair and who could have used more attention. All Spanish mothers were anxious to improve their English and this was a natural opportunity to hear it spoken and to converse."

The mothers commented in these ways:

"I loved the Family Room even in the beginning. (But) I was afraid to talk out and afraid they might call on me. This year I found a couple of Spanish girls and I felt more secure—that they are on my side. . . . I learned a lot there and felt much better about being there. I enjoyed most conferences and felt I could be myself. It is the only time to relax myself." (Puerto Rican parent)

"I regret not having spent more time in the Family Room. I enjoyed the discussions. I always learned something new." (Black parent)

There were also some critical comments:

"Some people don't want to sit around in the Family Room. They feel it is a waste of time or they are too nervous."

"I am not comfortable in the Family Room. There is a barrier between myself and the Negro parents." (Mixed-marriage parent)

---

* It was noted elsewhere in the report that this separation along ethnic and socio-economic lines was markedly absent in the discussion groups, where there was no subgrouping even in the choice of seating around the table.

"When there are projects, people relax more and open up more in their talk. Otherwise it is very loose there . . . I gravitate to other middle-class mothers. They are the most social and I feel relaxed with them. Not that they are the most illuminating or interesting . . . It is difficult to open discussions with other mothers unless you have an activity to do. It brings out a give and take. These are interesting."

The study goes on to comment:

"Only a few parents spoke about wanting to chat and gossip without doing something constructive. Two parents frankly admitted that they would have preferred not talking to anyone. One spent most of her time working in the classroom and the other tried to read but could not keep from entering into the almost always engaging discussions. . . ."

STAFFING THE FAMILY ROOM

The atmosphere of a Family Room is very much influenced, of course, by the personality, attitudes, and background of the worker who is in charge. In the Bloomingdale Program, this position was held by a succession of workers (Puerto Rican and black), who were chosen because they had some work experience that they could build on and who were also familiar with the community and more or less "indigenous" to it. They were identified as "family worker," "family assistant," or "family room aide."

The position of Family Room worker actually called for a variety of skills for which, as yet, there has been little formal training available. Ideally, it was thought that these workers should know children and families, be familiar with and accepting of people of all the socioeconomic and ethnic backgrounds in the community (especially the so-called "disadvantaged"), be sensitive to the special concerns of parents, and know the community resources to which families could be directed for help with their personal, social, and financial problems. They were to help in recruiting new families as vacancies occurred during the year or as a new program began each fall. They also were expected to serve as liaison between the parents and the staff. It was their duty to encourage the parents to express interests and needs for which educational activities could be set up. But more important, they were to be friendly, warm individuals who would make parents feel at home.

This was a large order and the salary that was available was in no way commensurate with these qualifications, even if persons with these capabilities were available. So persons were selected who had at least some of the qualifications. There was some turnover, largely because of changes in the workers' personal lives but, in general, the program was fortunate. They were a responsible and responsive group, who made the most of their abilities.

SPECIAL MEETINGS

As liaison, the family workers brought to the staff ideas that often became the substance of scheduled meetings on special subjects in the Family Room:

Early in the program a staff member of the Planned Parenthood Association came to discuss family planning. (While birth control information was eagerly sought by the mothers during the first year, by the third year they said they really weren't interested; now, they knew all about *that!*)

Representatives of the Welfare Department (now Department of Social Services) met with the parents from time to time to interpret their services.

So did spokesmen for the Welfare Recipients League, who came to tell parents who were on public assistance—and others, too—how the welfare system works and what benefits clients were entitled to receive.

A nutritionist from the Health Department talked informally about nutrition for the family; she spoke in practical, down-to-earth terms and gave suggestions for a balanced diet using low-cost government surplus foods. She also discussed low-calorie foods that can be bought at moderate prices, since many of these mothers struggle to keep down their weight. Later the mothers initiated cooking sessions, tried out her ideas, and shared their favorite recipes.

A police officer discussed safety precautions and how to cope with neighborhood vandalism, muggings, and other acts of violence—a source of increasing anxiety to the parents throughout the program.

And so special meetings continued, bringing in representatives of other organizations to discuss community issues as new problems were identified and new systems—like Medicaid—were introduced to deal with them.

DISCUSSION GROUPS

When the parent program was reorganized at the end of the first year, small, educationally oriented, on-going discussion groups became an important part of the plan. Prior to this, occasional parent meetings on special topics of child development and family relations had been given at irregular intervals. Since the parents naturally discussed their children whenever they came into the Family Room, a plan for a series of regular biweekly meetings on matters of parental concern about their children was now offered to the parents.* The mothers were interested but hesitant to commit themselves at first. Two groups were offered as an experiment, one for the Tuesday-Thursday mothers and the other for mothers whose children came to the program on Monday, Wednesday, and Friday. The meetings were to be led by the director of the parent program with the social worker whom they all knew participating as a "resource person." The leader would guide the discussion, contribute from her knowledge of child development and family relations, and pull together what came out in the meetings. From the very beginning, the staff in no way dominated the discussions. The sessions were based on the *parents'* concerns, *their* ideas and experience, which they shared with one another.

The attendance at these groups, which was purely voluntary, was remarkably steady and ranged from 11 to 15 parents at each session. It drew from all segments of the parent population, from white mothers (some of whom had been through college) to black mothers and Spanish-speaking mothers, some of whom had had only limited formal education.

The atmosphere was consistently friendly and frank, although there were strong differences of opinion. The parents spoke about the children and themselves without self-consciousness and showed they were deeply involved in their role as parents and in their concern for all the children in the groups. They also were concerned about their responsibility in community situations that affected their families. (The nature of the discussions and the diverse subjects they brought up are described in the next chapter.) At the end of these sessions, there was a general request that the discussion groups be continued and extended the following year, starting earlier in the fall.

The Yeshiva study reported on the response of parents to these groups, based on interviews conducted late that spring. More than half of the twenty-one parents interviewed felt the sessions had had great meaning for them; the rest felt they had some meaning, with the exception of one mother who felt they had little meaning for her.

Quoting from the specific comments of both black parents and white parents:

"Conversation in the Family Room is helpful but we never get into the roots like when the leader is there."

"The discussion was terrific. That is the best thing that ever happened. Just finding similarities in the families and children. The fact

* This was based on the experience of the parent program director in other similar settings.

that all children sass—something about the practical level of discussion. You find out more personally and about other people's attitudes. It was an eye-opener. . . ."

"I've developed more awareness of each of my children. That each child has his own thoughts. I'm talking more to my children. I'm finding out what they really think and what makes them happy. Like with eating. If they don't eat, they aren't hungry. Surprising, they really know."

". . . You start thinking about your children. It makes you observe your child more closely to see what the child really does. When other mothers bring up a topic, you think if your child has these habits and what you do about them."

In summary, a parent had this to say about the discussion groups:

"We wasted months before the program really got started in the Family Room. Both the white and black parents finally talked about sensitive problems. They, the discussions, have become more emotional but it has helped clear the air and plant a seed of trust."

THE PROGRAM REFLECTS COMMUNITY TENSIONS

During the third year of the parent project, the atmosphere in the Family Room gradually took a different tone. Following the wishes of the parents expressed in the spring, two parent groups met every other week in the fall. The attendance was good and the discussions were lively in the beginning. They dealt with some of the issues taken up in the earlier groups but explored them more thoroughly. And they brought out other poignant matters, such as the meaning of death to children—and to themselves.

Through December, however, the atmosphere in the Family Room seemed to change. Big preparations were under way for the Christmas bazaar, in which the mothers became more and more absorbed as the day drew near. They busily made hand puppets and many different articles to be sold—sewing, knitting, crocheting, each in her own special style. Gradually, however, the number of mothers dwindled; a smaller group of mothers—mostly white—took over, pushing hard for the bazaar to be a success. And successful it seemed to be, with many articles for sale and many parents helping in any and all capacities on the great day.

After the holidays a new tone burst through. Attendance at the discussion groups fell off; the sessions were stilted and slow, for no reasons that the staff could determine. Parents seemed restless and dissatisfied in other activities, too. So a general meeting was called in the Family Room to reevaluate the program.

The meeting was held, the room was crowded—and Pandora's box flew open. Excited words poured out, expressing with tears and considerable anger resentments that had been pent up and seething. They centered first around the preparations for the bazaar. There was too much bossing by the white chairman and committee members, said a number of black parents. They felt that they were being pushed around as a group. Their competence and skills were largely ignored, they felt, and they themselves were not given a chance or treated with respect. A few black parents disagreed and pointed out that pressures had built up because of delays; things just had to get done. But their comments were lost in the face of the bitterness that had piled up here as elsewhere as black parents struggled to find their own identity and demanded to be recognized. The white parents were stunned, especially those who had been most active in the bazaar. They began slowly to talk about their surprise and their total lack of awareness that they had ignored the black mothers. There was no apology but it was obvious that they looked back at what had happened to see if the criticisms were justified.

The discussion then turned to the Family Room activities. Here there seemed to be contradictory feelings. Some mothers—especially the more intellectually oriented white ones—said they felt the time there should be put to better use. They had had enough talk about bringing up children; there should be more planned discussions on serious social issues of the day. Yet, when they had attended, these same parents had taken part quite appropriately and had raised thoughtful issues that all the members had entered into, appreciating their comments. Others felt that, at times, too much had been planned; they wanted more free time to sit and talk and relax. As the talk went, it seemed as if all the parents were resenting anything that was planned on a regular basis, even though the subjects of the sessions were initiated by the parents.

The meeting went by so quickly, and the feelings ran so high that another meeting was scheduled for the next week, to sort out the many ideas that had been expressed and to think about the activities they wanted for the rest of the year. The parents and the staff felt that this had been an exciting, even disturbing experience for everyone, but that it was basically healthy and valuable. There had been no holds barred, and expressing their feelings openly seemed to release the parents' tension and freed them to talk together more quietly the next week and to make fresh plans. These included the scheduling of a new series of meetings on general topics of community concern and a new parent discussion group to be held for six weekly sessions, with specific registration. (For a sample schedule, see Appendix II.)

Twelve mothers registered. The attendance was steady and the group met in a separate room adjoining the Family Room. The discussions again covered matters of child-rearing but with increasing continuity and also with constant awareness of the impact of community conditions on the children, and of the parents' role in the community and especially in the schools.

These happenings are described in detail because they reflected the changing atmosphere in the community at the time. This was a period of increasing rebellion against all recognized institutions, the beginning expressions of the mounting crisis against authority. The weeks before had been filled with heated discussions of the plans for decentralization of the New York City schools and the ways in which these plans stirred up strong latent racial antagonisms. Not only in the schools but in planning for better housing, in antipoverty programs, in welfare and health services, everywhere parents were demanding a greater say in the services and institutions of the neighborhood. But they encountered endless frustration and their angry feelings seethed beneath the surface, ready to break through in unexpected ways.

In this program, the same forces were at work, confused by feelings that were not always relevant. But here there was a difference. Parents were listened to, in the long run, if not in every instance. They could talk out what they thought and felt; their ideas were given consideration and their feelings were respected. Even when there was strong disagreement in the group or between the parents and the staff, they could talk together in an atmosphere that accepted differences and that encouraged experiment and change.

It would be an exaggeration to say that differences were completely ironed out. The underlying lurking feelings of hurt and anger that cause many minority-group parents to react strongly under stress have had a long history in their individual and collective lives and, of course, cannot be resolved in such a limited project. But they were recognized and, to some extent, the group understood how easily they could be sparked by apparently unrelated events. Here, at least, small steps were taken to face the issues honestly and to see that, in this way, people could trust one another.

And so the tensions in the Family Room eased as parents worked together on a new footing.

Then came the shocking death of Martin Luther King, Jr. That night there was looting and burning in black Harlem, but the multiracial Bloomingdale neighborhood on its southern fringe was quiet. The following morning, black, white, and Puerto Rican mothers came crowding into the Family Room, under decorations that had been put up the day before for a long-planned cake sale. But the cake sale was largely forgotten. The groups were cancelled that day and mothers and children came to share their sense of bereavement, their shock, and their anger. Instinctively, they came to be with others in a moment of crisis and tragedy. It was as if they needed to reaffirm their faith that if real communication and community feeling can be achieved in one small interracial neighborhood, then perhaps it can one day be achieved in our larger society.

Of course, they did not talk in those terms. And despite the intensity of feelings shared by everyone there, there was some feeling of strain, some sense that the barriers between black and white could not be completely broken down, even under such stress. But they stayed together, talking, drinking coffee and, later, buying the cakes they had all shared in making. Somehow just being together seemed to help.

WHEN THE PARENT DEVELOPMENT PROGRAM ENDED: WHAT THEN?

The unity of feeling was put to a severe test during the next year, when the Ford grant had expired, the administrative staff was sharply cut back, activities for parents were sharply curtailed, and the program limped along on less than a shoestring. Selected Bloomingdale mothers, who became teaching assistants under the head teacher's supervision, assumed more and more responsibility in the classroom. And the Board became more and more actively involved in fund-raising and policy making. This they did with only a limited amount of assistance from the teachers. But some questions remained. Had the parents really developed the strength and understanding needed to carry on an integrated program as they had before? And had the parent program itself proved to be of sufficient interest and value to continue without much staff help? What about the Family Room as the center of parent activities? What went on there?

For the fall and early winter months the picture was discouraging. Nothing much happened. Only the coffee urn continued to glow, making coffee for the few who straggled in. (The rule that parents had to be on the premises if they were not needed in the classrooms was increasingly ignored.)

But, incredibly, again the picture changed. Two new parents ran the Christmas bazaar, which was the most successful one ever held. Other fund-raising and social activities were planned and carried through—another cake sale, a portion supper, a sale of specially designed Christmas cards, and an entertainment benefit. After the struggle in ideology and the renewed commitment to an integrated program, (discussed in Chapter I, pages 19–21) black parents, who were opposed to separatism, seemed to want to declare themselves, to prove that they, as proud black people, could do their share in making the program a success.

As we have seen, for a while some of the white families, who had been with the project for some years, had difficulty adjusting to this new attitude, but found new satisfaction as the total program began to pick up speed.

At first, little went on in the Family Room while these tensions seethed. Only later did the parents complain that nothing was being done; they found themselves looking back with nostalgia to the earlier activities of the parent program, even those who the previous spring had been most critical of it.

The new director of the project sensed their restlessness and decided that something had to be sparked, since the parents were getting nowhere themselves. She called the parents together, new committees were formed and, with the director's help, a calendar was set up for the spring months, based on suggestions given by the parent members.

Again the Family Room began to hum. There were innumerable committee meetings. Several cooking sessions were held in which the parents prepared interesting inexpensive dishes for one another (the tiny kitchen was jammed each time). The teachers demonstrated play activities—play dough, for example—that the parents could set up for their children on rainy days at home. A Bloomingdale parent, a nutritionist, showed a film and discussed the matter of introducing children to new foods. The parent education consultant from the Health Department held a meeting on sex education. Community leaders discussed several neighborhood action groups. There was interpretation of the current status of Medicaid. And there were other happenings as well.

Finally, the former director of the parent program, at the request of the parents, led four discussion sessions on parents' concerns about their child-rearing. These were well attended; all the parents, from different backgrounds, participated in a lively and productive interchange.

As the season closed, the parents went on record as wanting a strong parent program for the coming year.

By the following season, and the changeover to a full Head Start program, the parent program proceeded along many lines. Again, it was slow in starting and needed much support from the director, the family workers, and the parent committees. Many of the projects were extensions of activities that had been tested during the period of the Ford grant. Others, such as a ten-week High School Equivalency course, reflected the trend toward helping parents move up the career ladder. They included social affairs, such as a portion supper and a Hawaiian dinner at a restaurant; self-development projects such as language classes, sewing groups, and the like; involvement in neighborhood action groups, service on boards of several community organizations and agencies; fund-raising activities such as a Children's Fair; and recurrently, by request, meetings about aspects of child-rearing. For example, four workshops on problems of early childhood, again led by the former director of the parent program, drew a large response from parents of all ethnic, economic, and educational backgrounds. The discussions were lively and penetrating, and the exchange of ideas and reactions was rich and friendly. There followed a workshop with the consultant psychologist and a follow-up meeting with the teaching staff to share with them the concerns the parents had voiced in the workshops and to discuss the relevance of these concerns for the total program.

And while the emphasis shifted more toward career development and community problems, with less emphasis on child development in the early years, obviously the earlier experiences in the Family Room had borne fruit. Even the parents who were new to the program responded well. They seemed to have gathered out of the general atmosphere that the various activities there would have meaning for them, as they had for others before them. And so they got stimulation and satisfaction and a new kind of personal growth. Many, too, seemed to lose some of the feeling of powerlessness that had dampened their outlook, as they worked together—and saw results—for their children and themselves, the "school," and the community.

*   *   *

The story of the Family Room points up the fact that, to be successful, the program needs consistent direction. It calls for a capable family worker, whether fully trained or not (and where does one get specific training for a job like this?) who is well-organized and can follow through once projects are decided on. She must be able to listen, with an open ear and an open mind, to what parents have on their minds as they talk and work together. For it is from these ideas that activities can be planned to pick up their interests and enlarge their world. And she must have empathy with the parents and the natural social skills to make each one feel important and at home.

A few practical hints to those responsible for Family Room activities:

Consider a variety of projects, to meet different needs, and select only those that seem most in demand. It's better to go slowly, concentrating on a few and doing those well.

Don't undertake any project unless there is someone—usually a parent—who is competent to be in charge. Sewing classes, for example, must have a skilled person as leader. (Many parents hide such gifts under a bushel, but can be encouraged to use them to help others.)

Be ready to call on skilled persons to help where a good psychological background and knowledge of group techniques are needed to conduct a special project such as parent workshops or discusion groups. Leaders can be found in some social agencies or health and welfare departments, although it may take some searching to find an appropriate person.

Don't stay committed to a project if, after a reasonable length of time, it doesn't seem to catch on. One can always try something else the parents may be interested in.

Remember there are two possible purposes of programs for parents—those that give them additional skills for themselves as individuals, and those that help them function better as *parents* in relation to their children, at home, in school, and in the community. Both have their place in the Family Room. Parents sometimes get restless, however, if they stay too much with one or the other, and seem more satisfied if they take part in both from time to time.

When those in charge identify these two types of interest, they can help maintain a balanced program by suggesting different activities if the projects seem skewed in one direction too far, too long.

Chapter Four

Parents in the Discussion Groups During the Parent Development Program

Ten Bloomingdale mothers sat around a portable table at the rear of a small chapel in the church while their three- and four-year-old children were busily engaged in the play-groups in the basement. Two of the mothers had their younger children on their laps, eating cookies throughout the meeting; a third toddler played on the floor at his mother's feet. The mothers—black, white, and one Japanese—had moved to the chapel since they had found the Family Room too small for comfort at the opening meeting two weeks before. Also at the table were the leader (the director of the parent program) and the program coordinator who was also responsible for Family Room activities.

By this, their second meeting, the mothers were more relaxed. They had already found out what the parent discussion group would be like and were not stiff and anxious as they had been at first. They had had a chance to identify themselves, give the names and ages of their children—all of them—and say what they would like to talk about in the series of meetings that lay ahead. And, hesitatingly at first, but with increasing strength and frankness as they heard their own voices and listened to others, they had begun to list a variety of matters that they would like to discuss in the group. They already knew from the leader that the things they would discuss would relate to their children, of course, and to their daily lives with them. They also had been told, and had found out in the first session, that these meetings would not be lectures in which they would be talked at or preached at, such as they had often experienced in PTA meetings and church gatherings. Here they could really talk together about what *they* wanted and what *they* found puzzling or difficult—or pleasant and rewarding. They had also found that in talking about their children, they also were free to talk about themselves and how they felt about things. The leader saw that they talked to the point, more or less; she added to the discussion from her own knowledge of children and families; and she pulled together what they had all been saying so that it had extra meaning.

But, above all, they had found that they were all listened to, thoughtfully and with respect, no matter what they said. And they had already said some surprising things. At the first meeting in the small Family Room, they had begun by talking about some forms of their children's behavior that troubled them, "habits," they called them. They mentioned their children's nail-biting, lip-biting, the ever-present "security blankets" of the comic strips, and thumbsucking. In trying to see what these things meant to the children and why they turned to them, several mothers mentioned that the children's behavior seemed to run in families, and described cousins and sisters and brothers acting in the same way. Several mothers added that they remembered what they had done as children and how their parents had reacted. One mother added that she thought children picked up their habits from their parents. She said she had sucked her thumb as a child just as *her* child did now. Now that she is grown up, she finds she still puts her thumb in her mouth when she is upset or has trouble going to sleep. Out of all this came some ideas, underscored and restated by the leader, of the comfort and pleasure and easing of tension that children are looking for.

The second meeting, this time in the chapel, took quite a different turn. A white mother said she wanted to know how to explain race differences to children. The whole group nodded their heads in agreement and the discussion was off. The leader asked the first mother to say what had prompted her to bring this up. She told the group that her child had visited a white playmate who was being cared for by a black baby-sitter while the mother was at work, and had refused to do what the sitter asked, saying, "You're not my mother and, besides, you're black." The mother was very much upset that her child had seemed to feel superior because of her color. How, she asked plaintively, can I teach her not to judge people this way?

The other mothers then poured out many experiences that her question had touched off. One said her mother-in-law came from the South and is very prejudiced against Negroes; she doesn't want her to give these ideas to *her* daughter. Unaware of the extent to which she revealed her own biases, she said that the way to get over prejudice is to see the best in every race just as she sees the "darling Negro children" at her Sunday school; they are always the best dressed children and the best behaved; not like the "rough ones in this neighborhood who are the worst and make you feel afraid."

There was then a heated discussion as to whether the neighborhood was really any worse than other neighborhoods. Some of the mothers remembered gang fighting and ganging up against different minority groups in other parts of the city where they had grown up. But they had to admit that conditions in this area were bad in the schools and on the streets and that here it was usually black children who were thought to be the fighters.

At this point, a warm, outspoken black mother broke in with deep feeling. She felt she had to explain about the people in the neighborhood. They were tough, she said, because they were bitter—bitter because they were denied things that came easily to others. They pay high rent for poor housing, for example, as she had done before she got into a housing project. And they have a right to be bitter. Kids are robbed in the public school and a girl was stomped on. *"You* have to be tough, too," she said, and so she has had to teach her children to fight, to stick up for themselves. "I don't like to teach violence," she concluded, "but I don't want anyone to walk all over *my* children."

She described her own experiences growing up in a mixed community in the suburbs where things were as bad as in the South. In high school, the colored kids and the white kids ate at separate tables. Finally, some white students decided to join the colored ones. She remembers one boy saying, after he had gotten to know some of them, that he was surprised because he had been taught that all colored people were bad. She felt that such ideas were taught through the parents. Some colored parents teach their kids that all white people are bad, too, she added disapprovingly.

The group listened in silence and with sympathy. After a moment, they recovered and talked more specifically and in detail about how many of them had met situations of prejudice—as Jews, Irish-Catholics, Italians. The program coordinator, herself Negro, commented that times are changing; a few years back a Negro was ashamed to talk about his background, but that is not the story any more.

Gradually, the mothers built up a picture of the way patterns of prejudice were similar in a way for all minority groups, though there seemed to be a tacit agreement that the long heritage of oppression of black people was more severe than that of other minorities, and that they could not get away from their skin color. (As one of the mothers said in another connection, "You'll never know what it means to have a black face.")

The leader turned the discussion back to the children. What did they think and say about this? A young black mother said her son had asked, "Why is it bad to be colored?" She had answered that it was not bad; there were bad colored people and bad white people and people are good or bad regardless of color. Others told what they had done to help their children to understand the situation—and to have some pride about themselves.

The mother who had originally introduced the question said at this point that she was afraid she was not doing enough to help her child accept all kinds of people. She admitted that, having come from the South herself, she might be oversensitive and might overreact when her child refers to a person's skin color. Other mothers reassured her. They pointed out that children are often thoughtless and cruel because they don't understand, but that knowing children of all nationalities and skin color as *persons,* for themselves, as they learn to do at Bloomingdale, is the best way to break down the false ideas they may pick up from those who, too, are thoughtless—and uninformed. A white mother told the group with deep feeling that she was proud of her children. "They think for themselves and question us at home," she said. She described how she was brought up in a prejudiced home and hoped that her children would be better than she was. Besides, she added, she is amazed and pleased that her husband is helping; "he has not one bit of prejudice."

The talk then swung away from this emotionally-laden subject and moved on to children's reactions to anyone who looks strange; they mentioned children's curiosity about nuns, cripples, cerebral palsied children and—again—unusual skin color and how difficult it was to give them "answers" they could understand at their particular age levels. To which one mother said, in a rather muffled voice, "Sometimes answers are not enough."

Her comment seemed to reinforce what the mothers had said before, that it was the parents' attitudes that were important. The general feeling seemed to be that children need to be helped to accept themselves for what they are—black, white, yellow, or whatever—no matter what their life-situation. A black mother made a final comment. "Tell the truth, even if it is embarrassing," she said. "There is nothing to lie about."

After a few words of summary from the leader, the meeting broke up and the mothers left soberly in small groups to pick up their children in the playrooms downstairs.

*   *   *

All sessions were not at this high pitch, however. In all the groups, the mothers spent a good deal of time on problems of child-rearing that have preoccupied mothers from many cultural, ethnic, and socioeconomic groups in many places.

They brought up primarily the problems that called for some action on their part—weaning, for example, and what to do about several four- and five-year-olds who were still on the bottle when they went to sleep; toilet-training, still a difficult matter for some of the three-year-olds and an occasional four-year-old; thumbsucking, as mentioned before; sleeping problems, especially night-waking and wanting to be taken into their parents' beds; fears, including nightmares; and, to a lesser degree, their children's eating difficulties. There was some mention of masturbation, but these parents seemed to accept this as a natural phenomenon of early childhood, with the exception of the Japanese mother, who was so horrified when she found her child "playing with himself" that she could barely talk about it, much less mention the word "penis."

Much time was spent on these rough spots in their children's struggle to give up their baby ways and become more self-directing and grown-up. Without ever mentioning the words, there began to develop around and across the table a picture of how their different children were meeting the important "crises of growth," how they, the parents, felt about this and what they were doing and could do to make this all happen in a sound, healthy way.

Sooner or later—usually sooner—the groups turned to the question of discipline. This was a word that came up loud and clear; it seemed to be on everyone's tongues. But the mothers' ideas about it were confused. Usually they began by talking about what they did to get the children to do what they wanted them to—play instead of fight, be quiet instead of noisy, stop their pestering, especially when their mothers were on the telephone. And what the parents did took many forms. Some parents made frequent use of the strap (a number of them reported this without any particular feeling, other than repeatedly stressing the frustration that led them to it). Others believed in taking away a favorite toy, or keeping the children from looking at television, which was an important part of every family's home life, no matter what their economic status. Still others just refused to talk to the children, as a way of showing their disapproval. But these were all forms of punishment. Often the leader had to slow down the discussion and encourage the mothers to look behind the children's behavior to what the children were trying to tell them by the way they were acting. Then they could begin to think about the different approaches each of them might work out to help their children. For some it might mean spending more time with their children—if this were possible in their busy days; for others, it might mean directing their children into behavior that wouldn't get them into trouble, before the trouble started.

The matter of the telephone came up in a number of the groups, and almost all of the families had telephones. The children never seemed as annoying as when their mothers were enjoying a chat with a friend over the phone. The parents said they were mad at being disturbed, they were furious that their children had so little consideration—and on and on. Gradually they talked about the children's side of this and how it seemed to them that their mothers really weren't there with them, even though they were in the same room. One mother reported later that she hadn't thought about it this way at all before. Now, having the children's feelings revealed so vividly, she told her child when she was going to phone, set up something for her to be busy with and was much more patient with her.

But the parents admitted that they were often not only confused but inconsistent, caught between being too easy and being too strict, and not being sure when to do what. By experimenting with different ways and thinking about their particular children rather than general theories, they began to feel they would work things out better, little by little.

Neighborhood and community problems always came into the discussions, too. The parents talked about how hard it is to bring up children in close, crowded quarters, with everyone stepping on each other's toes. No wonder there is so much fighting at home, especially when the streets are dangerous, too; the young ones can't let off steam out-of-doors because their mothers like to keep them home, particularly toward evening when it gets dark. They talked, too, about their children's fears of many kinds and, repeatedly, fears of fires, with which everyone in the neighborhood was only too familiar. And in sessions of two different groups, held a week apart toward the end of the year, they discussed the impact of death on their children, although there seemed to be no immediate occurrence that precipitated their concern. How, they asked, could they help their children understand—and accept—what death means when they themselves were unsure and confused? They brought out a number of traumatic experiences in which they had lost someone close to them in their childhood and also as adults, and recalled vividly their feelings of being abandoned. They knew their children couldn't begin to understand the finality of death and would also feel lost if it hit close to them, unless they could help them. Perhaps the best they could do, they felt, was to assure their children that they would be cared for, no matter what happened. Despite their many different religious identifications and beliefs, their seriousness and concerns were strikingly the same. Their main thought was for the children.

Practical problems came into the discussions, too. How, for example, does one divide a terribly small budget to take care of what each child may need? And what do you do when one child really needs something more than others (a new coat for a teenager, perhaps) and the younger ones don't understand why they can't have one, too? And—most sadly—how can a mother cut herself up into pieces, as it were, to give each child his proper share—and still, as one mother said, have a little bit left over for herself?

As the groups went on, the character of the parents' interests shifted. They seemed to move away from the specifics of child care and management toward more thought about the values they held for their children, and the kind of lives to which they hoped they could lead them. At the same time, they talked searchingly about what the community offered—or did not offer—to help them. Obviously, their attention focused on the schools, which were under particular attack at the time, and what they, as individuals, could do to better the situation. But the tenor of the thinking shifted back and forth between immediate home problems and the larger community issues.

There is no time or space here to tell how these questions were met in the various groups. Sometimes the mothers gave suggestions that had worked for them; sometimes they gave one another sympathy and support. Always they tried to look deeper into their children and themselves to find the answers. Most of all, they gave each other the feeling that they were all in this together, from whatever background they came, struggling to be "good mothers" and knowing, too, that it is surely not easy to do so in these difficult times.

*   *   *

This, then, is something of what took place in the discussion groups of the parent development project. But here, as in other programs of this kind,* no two groups were exactly the same. Although parents seem to bring up many of the same general subjects, they do so from their individual vantage points, influenced by the immediate happenings with their very individual children and by the way their own personalities and temperaments respond to them.

The interplay between the parents is also never the same. The talk is determined, of course, by the ideas they bring out, ideas with which others are free to agree or disagree. But equally important are the subtle feelings that flow back and forth around the table—feelings of liking or dislike, of sympathy or irritation, and even of reserve until they know one another better. This project showed beyond a doubt that, as mothers get to know one another, these feelings cut across the lines of race or color or education or language. They flow out, both positively and negatively, in response to the way the mothers act and feel toward one another as individuals. By and large, parents found this the most significant part of the program, since it pulled together their experiences at home and what they were learning in the classroom. Often parents can integrate these two parts of their lives on their own. In these meetings they were consciously encouraged to do so—a process that was new for many of them.

* For more about the philosophy and techniques of leadership of such groups, see Aline B. Auerbach, *Parents Learn Through Discussion: Principles and Practices of Parent Group Education.* John Wiley and Sons, 1968.

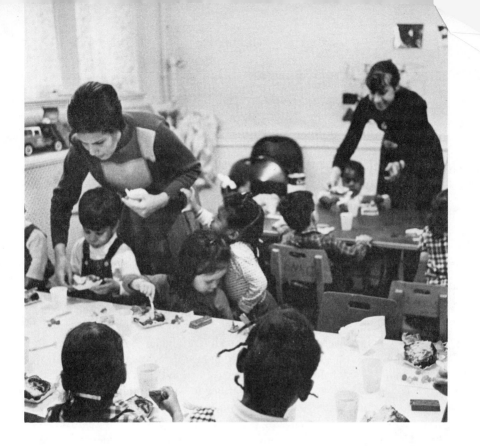

Chapter Five

How the Staff Was Helped to
Work with the Parents

The staff at Bloomingdale was an interdisciplinary and interracial group, representing many different levels of training and experience, and coming from diverse backgrounds. The composition of the group changed from time to time, as some moved out and others came in, but the general tone was maintained. These were dedicated persons—black, white, and Puerto Rican—as different from one another as one could wish, but somehow welded together because they cared about children and about each other. So the differences faded out—between professionals and parents, between one ethnic or socioeconomic group and another.

To make this possible, machinery had to be set up so that the staff could communicate with one another on a planned basis and could work out in practice the coordinated approach that was the distinctive feature of the Ford-supported parent program and of the Bloomingdale Family Program as a whole. The children's program was relatively simple. It provided a wide variety of "play" experiences that furthered children's general development while at the same time it gave opportunities for cognitive development at appropriate levels. More difficult to absorb were the many phases of the parent program—the parents' role in the classroom, their "educational" and social activities, meeting the needs of families for social work services, establishing appropriate contacts for the families with schools and community agencies—that were all part of this whole. Each part had to be understood for its own sake and in relation to all the others. For a diverse staff to absorb such a diverse program required frequent meetings—and constant interpretation.

Staff meetings were therefore set up on a regular basis. Here the staff shared information about special happenings, drew on their knowledge of each child and each family as they saw them, and talked about what they were trying to achieve from their particular vantage points. The administrators (director of the parent program, program coordinator, administrative coordinator), the teachers (professionally trained and relatively untrained), the family room workers and the community aides (with their various degrees of social work training and experience) all met on an equal basis and learned from one another. Parents came to these meetings from time to time—the chairman of the board, the chairman of class representatives, special committee chairmen and others—and they, too, learned while they reported their own part in the program.

Each one, staff member or parent, had a contribution to make. Sometimes it was knowledge of *a* child or *a* parent; sometimes some insight into a community problem that affected many of them, such as the parents' tension over a particularly dangerous traffic situation at a nearby corner; sometimes a comment that threw light on an attitude prevalent in an ethnic group, such as the strong feeling of some black mothers that their children should fight to defend themselves; sometimes a recognition of different styles of child-rearing that seemed to cut through the usual racial and class groupings and reflected much more the goals and temperaments of individual families. These contributions often came out indirectly in relation to a particular practical problem. But they added a great deal to the combined understanding on which individual staff members could draw.

There were some antagonisms among staff members, some competitive feelings and jockeying for position as plans were made for the staffing of the summer park programs and of the program itself year by year, but they were minimal. It seemed as if in most cases those best suited to do the work were selected—or almost selected themselves—for appropriate slots.

STAFF MEETINGS

Staff meetings were held weekly. Often they were exciting and stimulating. Sometimes—when they bogged down in the details of practical planning for classroom activities or trips, scheduling the parents to assist, and the like—they were pedestrian and dull. They were chaired by the program coordinator or, more often, by the director of the parent program. For this was the place where all the staff were able to fill in their background of knowledge of *parents* and to explore how this project could help parents build on their strengths.

Helping parents build on their strengths is still a relatively untouched area of interest in the training of professional people, although the word *parent* is everywhere. But parents are thought of (by definition even) primarily in relation to their children, rather than as persons in their own right. They are expected always to be there, always to be responsible for their children—as they have to be—but they are subjected to quick criticism and blame when things go badly and only rarely given credit or praise when things go well. So one of the basic purposes of the staff meetings that were not devoted to matters of procedure was to bring the parents into the foreground as individuals.

The staff meetings were conducted in much the same way as were the discussion groups. Everyone contributed and the sessions centered around immediate experiences with the parents that might add to the staff's understanding of the children in their groups. But the discussions moved beyond this to the parents themselves as they took part in the various phases of the project. The aim was always to encourage them in their development.

This called for the staff to do further thinking of their own attitudes. How did they view parents in general? Were they seen merely as appendages to the children—and to the program—who were to be used for different purposes? On these questions the teachers had some difficulty at first. In some who had been trained in early childhood education with its constant emphasis on the need for services—day care, foster care, or whatever—to pick up where families left off, there was a subtle undertone of downgrading the parents. They tended to see parents as incompetent, ineffectual; otherwise, why couldn't they do more for their own children? The burden fell on the teachers, they felt, who had to make up to the children for what their parents were not able to give them. This attitude was reinforced by the current stress on the need to supplement the experiences of "disadvantaged" children who were "culturally deprived."

Somewhat different attitudes seemed to come out as the program developed. The teachers and the rest of the staff saw that parents had much greater concern for their children than they had expected; they also were extremely competent in many unexpected ways—in the classrooms, in the Family Room, in organizing fund-raising projects, in writing and sending out newsletters, and so on; and they commanded great respect from everyone because of the quiet, steady manner in which most of them managed their crowded homes and limited budgets, took good care of their many children, and still found time and energy to help in the Bloomingdale Program.

The staff also brought out openly difficulties they had in working with and relating to some individual parents. The teachers discussed a number of personal antagonisms, primarily to a few parents who were bossy and driving and who, on occasion, were quite shrill about it in the classrooms and at meetings. They also were irritated by the few who promised to take on responsibilities and then never showed up. As happens in discussions in parent groups, talking about these problems eased the teachers' tensions a little and helped them to see the parents more objectively. With sympathy and support from other staff members, they were better able to work out ways of coping with the difficult things these mothers *did,* rather than merely being annoyed with them as persons. In their self-examination, the staff also admitted their having parent favorites. They felt that here, too, they had to watch themselves so they did not act either positively or negatively on these emotional biases.

Like the parents in class-group meetings, a number of staff persons expressed irritation with the families—mostly the families whose children were escorted—who had the greatest problems and who seemed least able to deal with them. Because of their feeling for the children, they wanted so much to have matters go better at home that, at times, they wanted to go in and *shake* the families to make them do what (they felt) they should. But they had to curb their impatience, while all the resources of staff were called on to see what could be of most help.

While these efforts were underway, however, there was no time to be lost as far as the children were concerned. As each year went on, considerable time was spent in talking about several children who seemed quite troubled and were in constant difficulty in their classrooms. Like all preschool programs, Bloomingdale uncovered a number of children with emotional problems and deviations in mental development, some apparently with an organic basis. But the percentage of such cases seemed to be about that of other similar projects.

Many of these children came from so-called "disadvantaged" homes where parents struggled against the overwhelming odds of large families, many without fathers, crowded quarters, limited finances, and all the social ills associated with living in an atmosphere of poverty. But some of the children with problems also came from more advantaged homes, where social and economic pressures were less intense. One could not generalize, of course, as to the causes of these deviations in development; each child had to be considered individually. The most troubled children from whatever background were referred to hospital or other child guidance clinics for diagnosis and (hopefully) treatment where necessary. But clinic resources here as everywhere were limited and waiting lists long. As in most preschool programs, it was recognized that there are nowhere near the services needed even to evaluate the nature of such children's problems, let alone provide therapeutic help if this is indicated. The program directed its energies toward giving them the best group experience possible, appropriate to their age and particular needs. While this was essential for all children, the program served to test the extent to which problem children can be helped through educational means. At the same time, and within the limited resources of time and available staff, it made what effort it could to modify to some extent the practical circumstances in the homes that make life so difficult for some of these families.

Here at Bloomingdale, procedures were flexible, and decisions were made in staff sessions as to what should be done in each case and by whom. There was no routine plan for home visits, for example, although it was the social worker or family worker who usually went into the home when special problems or situations came up. Sometimes it was decided that the teacher should see the parent by appointment, either at school or at home, to discuss something her child was doing at school and talk over what the mother might want to do to help. In one case, for example, a teacher discovered that a little "escorted" girl was confused and troubled about what was going on at home. Her mother was about to have another baby (her fifth) and the child was worried about who would take care of *her*. The teacher visited the mother, explained the child's upset, and encouraged her to talk frankly to the little girl about the coming baby. She stressed the need to assure her that she and the other children would be looked after while the mother was in the hospital.

The staff members—all of them—brought back to staff sessions reports of new information they gained in these contacts and reported their progress or failure in helping the families to cope with their problems. They were always aware that parents needed not only practical help but also a better understanding of the impact on the children of whatever crisis had struck the family. This was their educational responsibility in the Bloomingdale Program, to contribute where they could to the total educational environment of the child, at home and in the community, as well as in school.

TEACHERS' SEMINARS

At first, it seemed important that the entire staff attend each meeting, but in time the plan was changed to give the teachers more intensive preparation for working with their parents in the classrooms, in their parent-class-groups and in individual parent-teacher conferences. And so teacher seminars were held every other week, led by the director of the parent program; full staff meetings were held on the intervening weeks. As the year passed, the focus of the teachers' seminar became more clear. These sessions aimed to help the teachers in three ways: to help them become more aware of parents' concerns in general; to help them encourage the parents in their role as teacher assistants; and to develop group discussion techniques to use in their class-group meetings.

The content of the seminars shifted from one type of parent contact to another as the seasons passed. At first there was much discussion of how parents could be helped to fit into the classrooms. Soon, however, the teachers were concerned about having the parents learn more deeply the educational significance of the program. How could they underscore for the parents the meaning of children's play activities and help them see the possibilities for children's growth, for example, in the housekeeping corner or in experimenting with colors at the easels or even in fitting puzzles together with another child at the table? Could they sharpen the parents' observation of what the children were doing, so that they would be able to sense when a child was slowly finding his way with play materials and language and relating to other children or when he was stuck somehow and in need of a helping hand?

And so they discussed their different experiences in helping individual parents in the classroom to understand what they were doing and why. Sometimes, they reported, their contact was casual, spontaneous, as they commented to the parents in passing, suggesting something the mother-assistant might do to help a specific child or a group situation. Sometimes they talked at greater length with a mother who seemed troubled or unsure about what was going on. The teachers seemed to handle these contacts quite comfortably, after they thought about them. They had much more difficulty in meeting with the parents in their class-groups, which was the place, they felt, where the parents' participation could and should be worked through and given added meaning. The seminars then concentrated on the *content* of these brief sessions (the questions and concerns the parents might be expected to bring up) and some basic *techniques* of group discussion, through which the parents could learn from their experiences and from one another, at their own pace. (See brief summary, "Some Points to Bear in Mind in Developing a Discussion," Appendix III.)

Many seminar sessions were based on informal reports the teachers gave of recent class-group sessions. Teachers commented about what they thought had gone well and raised questions about what they thought could have gone a lot better. Their greatest trouble was believing that the parents would talk up. They were afraid they would have to start the session off with some kind of "spiel" about children, perhaps, or a formal interpretation of the value of a certain kind of play. With a little help, however, they found they could start these sessions informally, giving the parents the chance to bring up whatever they wished about the children or the day's happenings or classroom procedures. It was important, they found, that they, too, keep in mind—as they had to help the parents understand—that the specific purpose of these sessions was to focus on their classroom experiences as distinct from the parent discussion groups which many of them attended in the Family Room. The discussion groups covered a wider range of parent concerns about child development, child rearing, and parent-child relations.

Occasionally they reported that parents did find it hard to "get going" in class meetings. Sometimes they had so much on their minds they did not know where to begin. Sometimes they seemed to be blocked over something about which they had strong feelings. In no case, however, did they block altogether. The teachers became more skillful in helping them over the initial hurdle, and the discussions began to move. Before long the teachers completely forgot their fear that the parents would not participate actively in this type of meeting. Instead, their problem was how to guide the discussion so that all the parents would enter in in some way (and not have one mother monopolize the meeting) and also how to help them get something out of it in the short time they had together.

It was the time factor that caused most dissatisfaction, coupled with the fact that, though the parents seemed interested, the attendance at the class-group meetings was not as good or as consistent as the teachers would have liked. The meetings were held at the end of the morning, so the mothers who assisted that day could take part easily, but some others were apparently not sufficiently involved to make a special effort to come, despite advance notices and frequent reminders. The teachers felt—and still feel—that these meetings need to be given additional weight and support so that they can take their proper place in the whole educational scheme.

To make it possible for parents to come regularly, the meetings must be scheduled realistically, taking into account the parents' other duties and commitments.

The teachers must be convinced of their value, and be willing to work—and think—toward making them as good as possible. Otherwise, the parents too may feel that these sessions are not important.

The discussions must be live (and lively), giving free rein to the parents' reactions, questions, and comments.

And they must come to some point which the teacher either underscores or adds as an interpretation, whether it is a matter of a step in children's development or the meaning of social interplay in the group or the value of a kind of creative activity or whatever. Parents—and the teacher, too—need to feel that each session has come to some meaningful end, even if it seems to be a minor one.

As each season ended, however, the teachers found that the parents had really learned a lot in the discussions. The parents began to talk about changes they saw in the children's behavior as the months went on. They pointed out how much some of the rowdier children had settled down; that the attention span of the whole group had increased so that many of them now worked at a picture, for example, until they were quite satisfied with it; that their use of words had improved; and that they got along with the others much more happily with much less fighting. There were a few children, however, about whom the parents were concerned (and they did not hesitate to say so), children whose behavior stayed in a groove, without the shifts that ordinarily come as part of natural development. In most cases, these were the same children to whom the staff was already giving special attention.

Up to a point, the teachers shared with the parents their concerns and referred briefly to plans that were being made for individual children, where this was appropriate. The teacher had to move carefully, however, not to share with the parents more than a child's mother might want the parents to know. This situation was hard for the teachers and they went into it at some length in their seminar sessions. They became more comfortable when they saw that the talk in the class-group could be limited to what was clear to everyone from the child's behavior in the classroom. In this way, there was no risk of violating the confidentiality of what the parent might have revealed to the teachers or other staff members in a one-to-one relationship.

The later class-group sessions brought out some conspicuous changes in the parents themselves. The teachers remarked about parents who had lost their earlier shyness and who had begun to express their own ideas. They talked about mothers—and children—who were now "separating" easily, with scarcely a backward look. They found the parents more satisfied with the curriculum and more comfortable in fitting into it. And finally, the teachers commented on the open, friendly relationship that had developed between the parents across ethnic lines; they showed close feelings for one another as they worked together in the classrooms and in the class-group meetings. From their comments about visiting back and forth after school, it was apparent that the relationships extended far beyond the Program itself.

The teachers said they found a few mothers, however—but only a few—who seemed to have gotten very little out of participating in the Bloomingdale Program. They were mothers who seemed to hold themselves aloof from the other mothers and who thought in the beginning that they knew how the groups should be run better than the teachers did. Yet one of these very mothers, who had seemed one of the least involved, said she thought that the program was definitely understaffed and that it was unfair to put such a heavy load on the teachers. After a while she herself seemed more reachable and her child, who had made little obvious progress earlier in the year, suddenly began to shoot ahead.

In a program with as many facets as this one, it is impossible to determine the effectiveness of its various parts without elaborate research evaluation. Since this was not provided for in the project, the conclusions have to be based on observations and the thoughtful impressions of a conscientious staff and board. Their evidence suggests that the teachers played and are continuing to play a strategic role in the educational program for parents.

In the struggling years after the Ford Foundation project was ended, a good deal of the work with the teachers fell by the wayside. It picked up again to some extent when the program became a Head Start Center. Weekly staff meetings were held to discuss the children, the program, and classroom problems. Meetings with the parents of each group were scheduled to be held monthly, but often were skipped because of other pressing matters such as the children's health examinations. And no opportunity was provided to discuss these sessions on a regular basis or consciously to help the teachers develop group leadership techniques.

The new director, however, who had been a teacher in the days of the parent development project, made good use of the skills she herself had acquired. In conducting staff meetings and large parent meetings and above all in her contacts with parents, she put into daily practice the point of view and the skills of working with parents that had been at the core of the earlier seminars. Now they were part of her, in ways that she herself scarcely recognized. Undoubtedly, much of this was passed on to the teachers, through her leadership and personality, without their being aware of it. The flexible attitude of recognizing parents both as parents and helpers, with many levels of need, still persists.

One would hope, however, that in projects such as this, the staff's understanding of parents, their individual needs, and their possible roles in the program could be developed deliberately, as one of the important cornerstones of an early childhood program. This should include time for regular training seminars or staff meetings to explore important aspects of teacher-parent relations, the role of the teacher as model and guide for parents in the classroom and, beneath all this, the teachers' attitudes toward parents, generally and as individuals.

Undoubtedly, teachers have always played a great part in influencing parents. With more conscious effort, their potential for far-reaching results can and should be given its due weight—and status.

With only a minimum of in-service training and on-going supervision, they proved that they were able to work with parents as well as children, to enlarge their horizons and increase their confidence and competence. To do this, they looked at themselves critically and with growing self-awareness. And they were able to bypass some of their own "hangups" as they became more sensitive to parents individually and not as stereotypes.

This might not have taken place had it not been for the atmosphere of the project. Here not only the teachers but all the staff members were going in the same direction, despite periods of upset. Their feeling of unity and common purpose supported one another, and together they were able to accomplish with and for the parents what they would never have been able to do alone.

Chapter Six

Contacts with Families
Outside of School

Recently a Bloomingdale staff member received a call from a former mother living in the housing project. Could someone intervene, the mother asked, in a situation she had observed in her son's public school? She had spotted a youngster who seemed troubled and whose family needed help. What action could and should be taken? Together they decided that the public school guidance counsellor should be apprised of the situation and take it from there.

Two things seem significant about that small incident. First, that the mother was able to see beyond her own difficult life situation to recognize problems in others and seek help for them. Second, that she continued to look to Bloomingdale as the first source of that help.

Concern for others was built into the Bloomingdale experience, for the parents and the staff alike recognized that education did not begin and end at the schoolhouse door but was part of the child's total environment at home and in his community. Thus the social worker had many unofficial eyes and ears throughout the program. Whoever saw a problem—whether teacher or aide, administrator or parent—knew that there was an appropriate channel at Bloomingdale for dealing with it and that some kind of practical action would be quickly taken.

HOME VISITS BY SOCIAL WORKERS

In this brief report there is no need to describe in detail the kinds of social services that Bloomingdale tried to offer. The services are essentially no different from those provided by many Head Start and antipoverty programs, and consist largely of referrals to available social agencies, hospitals, clinics, psychological and psychiatric services, marriage and family counseling services, housing and relocation offices, job training and placement centers, and so on.

The need for such services was great from the beginning, and grew ever larger as the population of the program drew increasingly from more economically deprived segments of the neighborhood population. At the same time, the staff to handle social services became less adequate not only in number but in level of training as funds dwindled with the close of the Ford grant.

In their contacts with social and government agencies, the staff and the parents were constantly discouraged by the difficulties of the referral process. Invariably they were faced with long waiting lists and inadequate facilities. Often, parents who had agreed that they or their child needed help lost interest and gave up hope when faced with long delays. Even after a family had been seen (by a clinic or guidance agency, for example) it sometimes took many additional weeks to get back their report. In psychological investigations in particular, the end result too often was to have the clinic refer the child back to the program! No matter what the diagnosis, the clinic often requested that the child be kept on in the program, since there are almost no programs that can accept preschool children with special problems. And when in spite of the odds a disturbed child was finally placed in a special program, or a scholarship found for a bright one, everyone at Bloomingdale shared these triumphs and rejoiced.

What is of interest is not the kind or number of referrals that Bloomingdale made but the *style* in which they were carried out. In intervening in the life of a family, Bloomingdale itself served as an extended family from which many kinds of help could be obtained. The referral was only the first step. When the apointment was made, the social worker or an aide would accompany the mother to lend her support at least on the initial visit. In the meantime, arrangements would be made to provide baby-sitters for the family's other children, or óther parents might be asked to care for the children until the mother returned.

When a new baby was born, staff and mothers made sure that a carriage and crib and clothing were found. The social worker would visit the hospital to reassure the mother that things were going well at home in her absence. Sometimes the social worker made a special plea to an appropriate agency to provide a temporary homemaker to ease the family through the mother's absence; in other cases she would sit down with the mother to help her make her own plans for the difficult period.

When a parent was relocated to a new apartment and received a special welfare grant for furniture and household supplies, the social worker would help the mother plan her purchases and sometimes accompany her to the shops where she could get the most for her money.

Even when a direct course of action was not open, Bloomingdale could offer moral support and comfort. Illness or death in the family, continuing marital difficulties, or just the pressures of living with poverty day after day, were understood and appreciated, and the social worker made it a practice to stop in for frequent informal visits with many such families to whom she was a constant source of encouragement and support.

When the social worker made a home visit, she rarely went empty-handed. First she would go through the "clothing bank"—shoes and children's garments that had been outgrown and brought to the Family Room for others to use—and select a few items for the children.

Best of all was her home visit kit—a large coffee can filled with things for the children to play with: crayons, paper, scissors and paste, a book to read, collage materials, and play dough. This served a dual purpose. First, it so delighted the children that they would play happily and allow the grownups to carry on their conversation with few interruptions. But equally important, these were often the first materials of their kind available in the house. Some families did not provide even such basic supplies as crayons and paper for the young children, although these same families might buy an expensive (and quickly broken) toy at Christmas or birthday. Through the home visits the parents learned that inexpensive materials could keep their children happily occupied, and the social worker demonstrated how many things normally found around the home (such as old magazines, pots and spoons) were made to order for children's play.

For the mother who rarely participated at the school, this kind of home visit was a demonstration in miniature of what the children were doing and learning at the program every day.

OTHER HOME CONTACTS

Home visits by the social worker represented only part of the home contacts maintained by the program. If a child were absent from school for several sessions, a staff member or another parent would telephone or visit to learn what the problem was and to help if possible. Sometimes a sick infant was keeping a mother at home with all of her other children. Then a temporary escort service was arranged for the well children until the mother could bring them herself.

In addition to formal home contacts, there were dozens of informal and casual family contacts that took place all the time. Particularly when the weather was fine and parents were outdoors on stoops and project benches, parents took advantage of chance encounters with staff to bring up concerns they might never have raised at a formal meeting.

Then, too, since most of the staff members were neighborhood people, they often got together with Bloomingdale parents around other shared concerns, perhaps the public school where they might be parents together, or as part of a local community action group. This casual neighborhood contact tended to remove barriers to communication between the staff and the parents, and encouraged their easy acceptance of one another.

Parents and children also did a great deal of visiting back and forth. If two youngsters played well together in the group, the teacher might point this out to both parents, suggesting that it might be nice for them to see each other on nonschool days. Or the teacher might suggest to the parent of a shy youngster that she arrange for him to play with one of the other children in his group. Later, such visits took place naturally and spontaneously. In this way, many parents for the first time visited the homes of parents from very different backgrounds. Inevitably parents began to get together to share their child-care burdens. The fact that in 1969–1970 one-third of the mothers were able to take jobs was made possible by the number of cooperative child-care arrangements that sprang up at the program.

Parents also got together outside of school for committee meetings or to make preparations for some of the big fund-raising events and outings that Bloomingdale families enjoyed during the year. These events—the portion suppers, the cake sales, the boat trips to Bear Mountain—bring out the old parents and the new parents, present staff members and former staff members, children, husbands, and the whole family. In so doing, they bring home and school still closer together.

NEED FOR NEW MODELS OF SERVICE

We have already mentioned in Chapter Two how the presence of the escorted children in the playgroups created a paradoxical situation in the program: participation was nominally *required* of all parents, yet some parents really never participated at all. The same situation created a problem in the use of the social worker's limited time. Because the escorted children were generally members of families with many problems, there was always the risk that the social worker would be called on to spend the bulk of her time with only two or three families. One multiproblem family in particular, over a two-year period, required the involvement of the staff on so many levels that the staff members often felt torn between the immense needs of this one family and the equally valid, though less intense, needs of many other Bloomingdale families. Yet, even when there was really little response from this troubled family, the feeling of urgency around the family's and particularly the children's needs made the staff willing to extend itself still further.

In meetings of the staff and the Board of Directors, therefore, there was much discussion of the questions raised by the presence of escorted families in the Bloomingdale program. Is Bloomingdale the kind of program, does it offer the level of services, that greatly troubled families need? With its small social service staff, and its primarily educational setting, is Bloomingdale equipped to deal adequately with the multiproblem family, or does it offer no more than a brief respite for an overwhelmed mother and a few hours of healthy play and learning for her children? Although Bloomingdale's efforts were clearly better than no help at all, it became obvious as the Family Program Board discussed these questions that a very different model of service was needed to reach those families with overwhelming social and mental health problems. This model would have to be tied closely to the block and its life and it would have to offer many more services, virtually on a round-the-clock basis. The program that began to take shape in the Board's mind was called the "In-Building" Program* and was to be located in apartments renovated for that purpose on target blocks where families with many children were living under most unfavorable conditions. It would address itself to the needs of the families who seemed to be unable to take advantage of Bloomingdale or other community services. Services in the projected In-Building centers would range from an infant creche and nursery providing 24-hour day care, through prekindergarten and after-school programs, family and social activities, and comprehensive health and mental health care. Built into these services

* See Appendix VI.

would be training and job opportunities for the parents and other adults on the block.

Interest in the In-Building program was expressed in many quarters including the Office of Economic Opportunity in New York City, the Head Start office in Washington, and Yeshiva University which developed the detailed research component of the program. Although the proposal was never funded, its continued relevance is demonstrated by the ever-growing demand from inner city neighborhoods for adequate educationally oriented day care facilities, meaningful job training and placement programs, and more humane health care services, all within easy access of those who need them the most.

Chapter Seven
What Parents Learned

Parents—most parents—learn quickly when they see their children making use of new opportunities in new settings and when the atmosphere encourages them to observe the children thoughtfully. Much of what they learn they probably half knew already; in a program like Bloomingdale, these partial understandings were brought into the foreground. Parents looked at their children not only from their own personal point of view but also through the eyes of the teachers, other staff members, and other parents, with whom they had an on-going informal relation. And so their image of their own children was often challenged or added to as they tested it against what the children really were like and what they could or could not do.

It is hard to pinpoint the way in which this process took place. Parents responded in their own way, helped—or hindered—by how they viewed their child in the first place and the expectations they had for him. As one worked closely with the parents, however, one got an impression of *changes* in their understanding, changes that showed up in their behavior toward their own children and all children.

Many of these changes have already been suggested, as we described the functioning of parents in different phases of this project. *In summary,* these are the outstanding gains they seem to have made.

ABOUT CHILDREN

The preschool program that was at the center of the project emphasizes the children's physical, social, and intellectual and emotional development. It stresses growth in language skills and in creative expression through many forms of realistic and fantasy play, while at the same time it gives children freedom to take part at their own pace. In a final class-group meeting at the end of one season, the parents noted many changes that had taken place during the time the children had attended the playgroup. The following comments by the parents are taken verbatim from the teacher's report of that meeting:

> ". . . the children's increasing awareness of each other. Specific relationships with certain children (some children build together, others look at books or listen to records together and others join in imaginary play, etc.). Relaxed and happy atmosphere: this has stimulated an un-inhibited flow of conversation along with a sense of humor. . . . understanding that everything is shared. Willingness to wait for turns, because there is security in knowing that every child will get a turn. Increased attention span. A very real recognition that children learn when they enjoy themselves. Appreciation of lack of pressure and realization that children grow in different ways, at different speeds, dictated by their needs and interests. . . ."

Seeing their children along with the other children, the parents built up a picture of normal child development into which each child fitted in his own way with his own individual variations. This gave the parents a general yardstick of growth which the staff helped them to use with discrimination. They came to appreciate a child's steps forward and were sensitive and thoughtful in picking up when he failed to progress, exploring the possible causes for such a delay with the help of all available resources.

Parents also came to hold more realistic expectations for their children and other children. The parents who tended to control their children's active play came to accept a little more easily the children's boisterousness, messiness, and noise, and even put up with this kind of behavior at home—within limits! Others, whose children tended to be quiet, passive little ones, began to encourage their children to be more active and aggressive and to speak up. In one case, a mother was troubled at first when her shy, considerate three-and-a-half-year-old daughter began shoving and grabbing; she put up with this behavior and saw that it was a healthy step in her development, but later she admitted that she was relieved when the child went back to being more generous and thoughtful of others.

Against the overall picture of child development as it applies to all children from whatever background, these parents seemed to loosen up their ideas and expectations and were a little better able to accept the diversity that is inevitable in any group of children. The extent to which this diversity comes from hereditary factors or from environmental influences—interpersonal, social, cultural (such as different group standards of behavior), or even physical (such as nutrition)—is difficult and usually impossible to determine. But it is there. When parents recognized it, they tended to ease off in pressuring their children to conform rigidly in their behavior. They did everything they could to help a child develop to the best of his capacity, whatever it was, and to reinforce his natural push to grow. They were pleased when they saw a child's individuality come out when he was free to experiment and to express himself spontaneously.

ABOUT THEMSELVES

For parents themselves the most obvious result of taking part in a project like Bloomingdale was their greater confidence in dealing with children singly or in small groups, not only at school but at home. In many families, mothers who rarely had asked other children to the house because they found it a chore, began inviting children in the afternoon, several at a time. A "group" of children no longer terrified them. In a way, this called for them to be more active with the children, at least in keeping a watchful eye on them, but they found the time went quickly—and usually more happily for everyone, despite moments of fighting and temporary disruption. And the house was not *so* pulled apart that it couldn't easily be put together again, with the children's help. As they took more initiative in this way, they felt more confident of themselves, without even thinking about it.

What is more, they began to be more accepting of themselves in these new situations, readier to know what they could do easily and well and what they really didn't like to do—and probably did badly. There were enough opportunities in the program so they could pick and choose, up to a point, and not feel guilty if they didn't all take on the same responsibilities. Assisting in the classroom was, of course, required of everyone to some degree. But once their minimum stint there was done, they didn't *have* to fill in for another mother if they didn't want to. If they preferred, they could make things for a bazaar in the Family Room instead, or put the newsletter together or just fold notices and stamp them.

They got most satisfaction, however, when they really took an active part in running the program as an officer or board member, and saw that their efforts really paid off. Sometimes it meant sharing in decision-making about new quarters, fund-raising, or the selection of staff members. Crisis after crisis was solved almost miraculously when the parents really got to work, and the program not only continued but expanded in new directions. No wonder that such experiences gave the parents a sense of power, and emboldened them to make their voices heard in the community. And heard they were!

Such growth in competence and self-confidence has important mental health implications. It tends to break down some of the overwhelming sense of powerlessness, of hopelessness which many families who live in disadvantaged neighborhoods such as the Bloomingdale area so often experience. Here, knowing that by their own efforts they could create better opportunities for their children, they began to feel that they might not be so helpless in changing other aspects of their lives. Thomas Gladwin has suggested that helping black and other minority people overcome their sense of utter powerlessness may be done through self-help programs developed out of the felt needs of the people.* This is the approach of the Bloomingdale program; in this lies a large measure of its success.

More personally, parents said they felt less isolated, less alone in dealing with their children. There was a strong feeling of solidarity that came from working side by side with other people from different backgrounds, who helped one another in minor crises at school and often had suggestions about personal and neighborhood problems. (Or at least gave a listening ear and sympathetic support.) So much did parents feel that they were a part of this small working community that it was they, more than the little ones, who were sad when their children went on to kindergarten or first grade. It was *their* tears that literally flowed the last day of school.

For individual parents, the project had been an oasis (as one parent expressed it), a place where they could be themselves, protected for a few hours from the buffeting of outside demands. Here they could forget themselves in their absorption in children. For some, it meant even more. In at least two cases, mothers said it had helped them ward off depression. The staff was keenly aware of the psychological struggle of both of these

* Thomas Gladwin, "The Anthropologist's View of Poverty," *Social Welfare Forum.* New York: Columbia University Press, 1961, pp. 73–86.

mothers and had plans ready to refer them for intensive casework or treatment services if it seemed desirable. In both cases, however, it seemed that their intense participation in the program gave them time to mobilize their own resources—at least for the time being.

Others, too, were supported through difficult, even tragic periods—the death of a family member, marital discord, and divorce. (Each year there were a number of separations and divorces in Bloomingdale families.) One mother said she couldn't have lived without Bloomingdale when her husband died suddenly. In her own words, "It helped me keep my sanity." Another mother, recently returned to the city from abroad, where her husband had been given a several-years' work assignment, was so disenchanted with conditions in this country and with the unfriendly, selfish, inconsiderate behavior of the people in the neighborhood that she felt defeated and lost at every turn. She poured out her dissatisfaction in one of the discussion groups, documenting her impressions with specific cases in point. Gradually, she regained her composure, slowly made friends within the school group, and even began to smile.

And a Puerto Rican grandmother, responsible for bringing up a charming but difficult little girl, was eager to help in the program but was shy because of her poor English. She, too, found her place in the classroom, primarily because of her love for children. But more important, she gained confidence in herself to the point that she talked freely to her neighbors in the housing project, mobilized her natural feeling for people and began referring them not only to the Bloomingdale Family Program but to the Conservation Office closely affiliated with it, where she knew people could get help with a variety of housing and community problems.

These are a few of the success stories, stories of parents who changed quite dramatically during their contact with the program, apparently as a result of their experiences there. Undoubtedly there was a process of self-selection which motivated certain families to come in the first place, either because the program gave them what they wanted for their children or because they were in sympathy with its goals and atmosphere. This meant that, in general, they were inclined to be favorably disposed from the beginning. But certainly there were others for whom the contact was not so favorable. Occasionally they said so, sometimes they took their children out of the project and placed them in other school settings. But this happened rarely.

Probably the most spectacular learning such a project gives parents is the chance to get acquainted with families whom they would never know otherwise. Here in the close association of a racially mixed parent body and staff, all with different experiences and ways of life, parents from all backgrounds found that many current stereotyped ideas and assumptions about "groups" and "classes" of people just weren't true. Black people, they saw, were not disinterested or ineffective—as a group—any more than whites. Whites weren't always bossy and superior. Black and Puerto Rican parents are just as eager for a good education for their children as any others. And so on. In general, they found that, by and large, white, black, Puerto Rican, Japanese, and Chinese parents all have similar goals for their families: quality education, decent housing, and better opportunities for all adults as well as children.

They learned too, that there are positive values they hadn't recognized in some parental attitudes they had been quick to criticize. Learning from and listening to one another seemed to make them slower to judge and readier to accept that there are many ways of meeting life's demands. Here at least, freedom to speak freely and to exchange ideas seemed to loosen parents' minds and shake their rigidity. They developed new relationships, new friendships, which, in turn, brought new insights and they found themselves moving more easily in an expanded social world.

PARENT PARTICIPATION LED TO
COMMUNITY LEADERSHIP

Since 1965, in New York City and throughout the country, parents have moved into many areas hitherto reserved to professionals. Neighborhood people have begun to take leadership in community action. Paraprofessionals are showing their value in the public schools and child care programs. Family assistants have become part of the social service team, as have health aides in the public health services.

How do communities identify and develop workers of promise and ability? The Family Program provided some clues, for an interesting development of the program was its evolution within the community into an informal training institute for neighborhood workers.

In the program, many parents began to see themselves for the first time not only in relation to their own children but in relation to other families as well. Nor was their concern limited to educational matters or problems affecting Bloomingdale's small circle of families. Just as the home and school environment was seen to affect each child's development, so the total community came to be recognized as a part of every child's environment for growing and learning. More specifically, the same experience and training that prepared Bloomingdale parents to take responsibility in the program also prepared and encouraged them to take responsibility in other settings. As a result, a high proportion of Bloomingdale parents and alumni are found in leadership roles in other neighborhood programs, as staff and volunteer workers.

As these parents move into new settings and new responsibilities, they bring something of Bloomingdale with them in the way they interact with other parents and with children and teachers. This kind of outreach was spontaneous and unplanned. But it was probably inevitable. For as the need was growing within community agencies for indigenous workers to relate to parents and children, Bloomingdale proved to be one of the very few neighborhood programs preparing parents for this role.

As parents brought back to Bloomingdale word of what was happening in the neighborhood, the Family Program felt the need to reach out into the community in a new way. At one point, Bloomingdale inaugurated a deliberate, although limited, effort to bring together the many agencies in the community that work with parents and children to explore ways of establishing better lines of communication with parents. In the spring of 1967 Bloomingdale set up a community seminar on "Reaching and Involving Parents in Neighborhood Programs." The director of the parent education project acted as discussion leader and invitations were sent to representatives of established institutions and community action groups.

Attending this seminar were the principals and the guidance counsellors of the five local elementary schools; presidents of parent associations in the public schools; public health nurses; the social work consultant to the neighborhood's Maternal and Infant Care Project; several family assistants in Head Start and other preschool programs; and representatives of local action groups. Seven discussion meetings were held that spring. Most of the sessions were concerned with communication: How can the agencies communicate with the parents? How can the parents make *their* needs and wishes felt? The parent representatives claimed that black and Puerto Rican parents were discriminated against and were made to feel unwelcome not only in the schools but in the traditional parents' associations as well. The school principals were defensive, at least at first. They complained that the parents did not appreciate how hard the schools were working for their children. The participants spoke frankly and often heatedly, and although they used common terms, it was evident that words—such as "parent participation," "acceptance," and "involvement" —had quite different meanings to the participants around the conference table.

At the end of the series of meetings, the participants recognized that they were just beginning to communicate with one another and asked that the seminar continue the following fall. But when the participants reconvened after the summer, a totally new feeling gripped the community. School decentralization was in the air, the Bundy report had just been issued, and the local Joan of Arc School complex was being talked about as one of the possible demonstration districts. Although the school administrators were far from supporters of the present school system—they had many complaints about how the system restricted their own freedom to experiment and innovate—they expressed many fears of decentralization. Where they had talked of parent involvement the previous spring, now they hinted at "power groups" and "power plays" that they feared would vie for control of their schools.

Nevertheless, even in this climate of anxiety, the series of meetings between the community and its institutions seemed to have been of value. Meeting over a period of time had brought most of the participants closer together. Now they were able to discuss burning issues more quietly and thoughtfully. At least they listened to each other, even when they could not agree. Also, even the school principals could recognize that the ferment in this community was creating among parents more interest and concern than ever before in the school and in their children's learning. And the parents felt that here at least their voices were being heard.

BLOOMINGDALE'S IMPACT ON OTHER PROGRAMS

While the parents found themselves interpreting Bloomingdale to the neighborhood, the staff brought word of the program into the larger community. As strongly attached to the program as the parents, they took advantage of opportunities to share their experiences at professional meetings. In 1968, for example, the director of the parent education project presented a paper at the 45th Annual Meeting of the American Ortho-Psychiatric Association in Chicago.*

When the staff moved on to other roles in other programs, they were eager to make use of the Bloomingdale experience in their new settings. In turn, the Family Program received many visitors who came to observe the program in action. Head Start personnel, the staffs of mental health agencies, teachers and students sent by the Ford Foundation and by the universities with which Bloomingdale was working at that time—all came to the program and created an exchange of ideas that was productive on both sides. Within the playgroups, teachers who had once felt shy even about having parents in their classrooms, ultimately became inured to important guests and professional visitors.

These many contacts may have influenced other programs to some extent. The evidence, however, cannot always be measured directly. "Influence" is a vague term, at best. Furthermore, this is one area in which members of the Bloomingdale family are not objective. But they do see reflections of the Bloomingdale Family Program in many places and many programs, and they know the resemblance is not accidental.

* Aline B. Auerbach, "Parent Development Through Active Involvement with Their Children in an Integrated Preschool Education and Family Program." (Unpublished Manuscript.)

Chapter Eight
What Others Can Learn

What can be learned from what happened in the Bloomingdale Family Program?

First, *that where there's a will there's a way*—if people care enough. It was the singleness of purpose shared by a group of devoted parents and staff members that kept the project going, and going ahead. The goal was clear—an integrated preschool experience for their children, in which parents participated in every part and assumed responsibility for its operation. The commitment to this goal enabled the program to survive through one financial crisis after another, to add a creative pioneer parent development project that gave it additional substance, and to weather a strong movement toward the separating of blacks and whites that for a short time threatened its survival.

The lesson is that a project of this kind can succeed if the people who are involved understand its goals, are committed to them and are willing to work to make them come true.

The parents all found their special places in the program because *it was administered flexibly and cooperatively,* taking into account the personalities and preferences of the parents as people.

In such projects all parents can not be expected to perform in the same way or at the same degree of intensity. Programs are successful if they are based on realistic expectations of the varied levels of competence and performance of parents from many backgrounds who happen to come together, and for whom, at first, the only common denominator is their wish to have a program of this kind for their children.

Good will and a common purpose, however, are not enough. At Bloomingdale it was evident that *there had to be skillful, experienced, sensitive people in both parts of the program*—the children's program and the parents' program. Unfortunately, training and experience are not always accompanied by the special kind of sensitivity such a project calls for. In one instance, for example, a white program director who was thoroughly expert and experienced in early childhood education and who had worked with black and Puerto Rican children, was not attuned to the varied reactions and needs of many different parents, nor was she really comfortable in working with those families who came from class and cultural groups different from her own. Her sincere attempt to work with them "without prejudice" unexpectedly made her seem condescending and patronizing. She seemed to realize her own inadequacy and stayed with the program only a short time.

Members of the staff of such a project should be mature, warm persons who are at ease with people as people. They should be aware of their own biases, and willing to develop more self-knowledge, as members of an interracial, interdisciplinary team of professional, semitrained, and untrained workers (many of whom are also parents).

How can such persons be found? We have already discussed the shortage of personnel trained in the various skills demanded by such a project, who are able to relate to children *and* parents of many races and cultures. All the usual employment sources were tapped to add to the staff when needed—both governmental and private employment services; the placement offices of academic, educational, and social work training centers; consultants in various city departments who were in touch with preschool projects; and, always, personal contacts. Once found, persons had to be evaluated individually, always expecting that some mistakes of judgment would inevitably be made. Here we found mistaken judgment in both directions. Whereas a few persons turned out to be less flexible and effective than was expected, others adapted themselves well to this unusual setting and drew on unsuspected reservoirs of sympathy and empathy with children *and* parents, adding a whole new dimension to the character of their previous work as teachers or social workers or administrators.

The selection of personnel for such a project is difficult and critical. Persons responsible for making the choice must expect some disappointments. Professional training and experience is essential for key teaching and social work positions; often fully qualified workers may not be available, in which case one has to turn to partially trained "subprofessionals," or as they are being called, "paraprofessionals." These workers, usually chosen from the neighborhood, can contribute to the program their special knowledge of the people in the area and the problems they face in the community. (There are many opportunities today for paraprofessionals to take part in training for career development, and every effort should be made to release them for the necessary training time.)

Whatever their present technical qualifications, persons should be chosen for their attitudes toward people and warm, human qualities. For if they are unable to accept and respect parents as well as children for what they are, they can never help them to learn and grow.

Whatever they bring to the project, all staff members must be given a chance to supplement their skills through in-service training in the areas that may need strengthening, especially in relation to parents. As suggested in Chapter Five, this may mean, for some, broadening their understanding of parents, or a wider exposure to the characteristic life styles of different nationality or cultural groups for others. It may also mean developing new group skills in working with adults as well as children, and refining their interviewing techniques, using them toward educational rather than treatment goals.

What light has this program thrown on *developing better intergroup relations?* We have said again and again that better relations between different ethnic and social groups have come about through having parents and staff members work together in any and all parts of this undertaking, but with certain limitations.

Realistically, good relations can be expected to emerge in any similar project in which people have a purpose that has deep meaning for them, and in which a healthy atmosphere is set and maintained by those in responsible positions, both the parents and the staff.

To be equally realistic, however, one must expect, also, as here, that *the atmosphere may change under the influence of new pressures in the community.* We have seen how at Bloomingdale such pressures threatened at several points to undermine the structure and purpose of the program.

This experience suggests that those in charge of such projects must be sensitive to a change in the atmosphere of a program, must open the way to find what is causing such a shift, and change procedures, if necessary, in order to meet the needs of those involved more satisfactorily.

Probably the most important single step in such a reappraisal is the need to encourage the participants to speak out, to say what is on their minds and what they are feeling, even though it may be unpleasant or painful.

There is no doubt that this program would have been more thoroughly effective for the families whose lives it touched, if *complete social work services* had been available, with a steady reservoir of trained professional workers, and ready accessibility to diagnostic and treatment facilities.

The availability of such services can unquestionably further the outreach to the poorest families in difficult neighborhoods—families that are poor not only in financial resources but also in their ability to cope with the overwhelming personal and social problems so many of them are facing.

In setting up any kind of preschool program, these services should be built in from the beginning, both for the children and their families.

Finally, there is a great need for a *pooling of information about new types of work with parents* in all kinds of settings. Here, we learned what we could from professional reports in the literature and at conferences and from individual contacts, but the knowledge was hit-and-miss.

Much more attention should be given to exchanging experiences and honestly describing the relative successes and failures of different projects and approaches. It might even be possible to set up a clearing house on parent activities, under government sponsorship at federal, state, and local levels.

Along with this must also go *improved methods of evaluating the effect of programs such as this,* as seen in educational gains and changes of attitudes. It takes complex procedures and fine skills to measure results of this kind, and evaluative research is not only time-consuming but costly. Many projects have had to settle for measuring a few variables—or none at all—depending, instead, on careful reporting and the thoughtful impressions of conscientious observers and staff.

But if this field is to be expanded as it should be, it must be accompanied by intensive evaluative research. Then it will have a strong, sound foundation.

Even without such scientific underpinnings, there is growing evidence that parents have great capacities, even under the most adverse conditions, if they are given a chance in an atmosphere of mutual learning and respect.

There is room for much experimenting in parent education and development. Many approaches should be used to encourage parents to go into activities of many kinds related to their children, where their interests naturally lie. Much more thought must be given to helping them look at the meaning of these new activities not only for their children but for themselves. We believe that this calls for multidisciplinary staffs whose members have acquired, through training and work experience, a special awareness of parents' strengths and limitations, and are able to step in when parents need them to extend their vision and understanding. Parents are entitled to the thoughtful help and conscientious, honest support of people who care.

Appendices

Appendix I

A handy guide for the Playgroup Parent
with useful and interesting information on:

1. The Bloomingdale Program for children and parents
   ...how it all began...what it stands for...what
   its aims are.

2. Basic Playgroup Information...school hours...holidays
   ...registration...where to park your strollers...and
   other odds and ends.

3. Basic Information about Parent Participation...in the
   classroom...the Family Room...working on committees.

4. Practical Hints for classroom assistants...suggested
   routines for helping in specific areas...the block
   corner...the housekeeping area...paint corner...
   workbench and water play.

5. General Guidelines for working with the children...
   how we help the children learn...coping with the
   uncooperative child...when to step in.

6. How mothers and teachers feel about working side by
   side in Playgroup...a Playgroup mother and a teacher
   write about their experiences in the program.

1. THE BLOOMINGDALE FAMILY PROGRAM FOR CHILDREN AND PARENTS

What has the Bloomingdale experience meant for our children and ourselves?

* A chance for our children to play and learn together.

* A chance for us to know our children better through sharing their preschool experience.

* A unique opportunity to see our child at first hand as his teacher sees him...to observe the way the teachers work with our own and other children...to help the teacher see the child through the parent's eyes too.

* A chance to know our neighbors through working together in an integrated community program.

* And finally, a chance to get together with other Bloomingdale parents and the staff, to discuss the issues that concern all of us—problems of everyday living with our children, schools, housing, health care, parks and recreation—and to seek forms of action for making this community a better place for all of us to live in and bring up our children in.

2. BASIC PLAYGROUP INFORMATION

Location:

Once again, Playgroup is divided between two locations this year. Luckily they are very close together. Last year's parents will also be happy to note that while the two locations may be a few steps apart, there are no stairs to climb this year!

The three-year-olds and four-year-olds—including Marion Borenstein's 5-day group, and Susan Feingold's and Joan Sandler's 2- and 3-day-a-week playgroups—will be together at 240 West 102nd Street.

The Family Room and the Toddler Room will be together at 868 Amsterdam Avenue, where the mothers and the little ones can keep an eye on each other.

School Hours:

The Playgroup day begins at 9:15 in the morning and ends at 11:30 AM. Children entering in the morning should use the side gate which leads directly to the school entrance. The children will be dressed and ready for dismissal at 11:30.

Coming on time in the morning is important not only for your own child's happiness but for the well—being of the entire group. A child who comes in late misses out on activities, instruction and a smooth unhurried start of his school day. Latecomers also disrupt the entire group and mean that the teacher has to interrupt what the others are doing to bring the latecomer into the group.

Because the outside door opens directly into one classroom, it is necessary to avoid a parade of late arrivals going through this room every morning. The outside door will therefore be locked at 9:30 every morning. Children coming after 9:30 will have to use the apartment lobby entrance.

Holidays:

Playgroup is closed on all holidays on the public school calendar. If the public schools are open, we are too. If the schools are closed, so are we.

Strollers and Carriages:

Bikes, carriages and strollers should be parked inside the side gate that leads to the school entrance. We will keep a large tarpaulin handy to cover them with, in case of rain or snow.

Carriages should not be brought into or left in the main lobby of the apartment building. If you come late, park your carriage in the yard first, then bring your child in to school through the lobby entrance.

We recommend that you purchase a simple bike chain for your carriage so that you can leave it out in the yard without worrying about it.

Forms and Records:

Two forms are required for Playgroup families:
  1. An Intake form, listing addresses, phones and basic family information.

2. A Health Record for each child in the program. Your doctor or the Health Station can complete this form for you, listing innoculations and pertinent medical information.

When a Child is Ill:

If your child has to be out of school due to illness, please tell the teacher or the office. Particularly where a communicable disease—like mumps or chicken pox—is involved, other mothers would like to know what to expect and when to start looking for bumps, spots or swellings on their own children.

Birthdays:

A birthday celebrated at school is an exciting event for any youngster. But please, mothers, keep it simple! Let the teacher know in advance, and together you can plan a celebration that will be fun without being elaborate or overwhelming.

The Playgroup Program:

Playgroup operates under special Health Department regulations under which each mother (and not the school) retains responsibility for her children while they are at the program.

As schedules of participation get organized, two mothers will be assigned to assist in the classroom each day. The other mothers are expected to be in the Family Room, where they can be "on call" if they are needed by the children or the teachers.

Emergency Escort Service:

Generally speaking, every mother brings her own child to Playgroup. However there are times when a mother is ill, or another child in the family is sick, and a mother is not able to bring her child to Playgroup.

We plan to organize an emergency escort service to help out on these occasions by bringing a child to Playgroup when the mother is temporarily unable to do so herself. The Group Chairman of your child's class will be the mother to contact if you need this service.

Dues:

Membership dues in the Bloomingdale Family Program are $1 per year. Families are encouraged to give whatever they can to keep the program going.

3. BASIC INFORMATION ABOUT PARENT PARTICIPATION

Bloomingdale's uniqueness lies in the fact that parents
participate in every aspect of the program—from helping in the
classroom to serving on the Board of Directors and making policy
and plans for the entire program. This program is based on your
participation. We not only welcome your help, your talents and
your ideas...we need them and cannot function without them!

In the Classroom:

All of us take turns assisting the teachers in the classroom.
For most of us, this works out to two or three mornings a
month.

Each group has its own "Group Chairman" who works out a
schedule with the other mothers and assigns them on a
rotating basis. If you can't be at Playgroup on your day to
assist, call the Group Chairman and she will arrange for you
to switch days with another mother.

Of course, some mothers are able to put in more time in the
classroom, some mothers are there less often, and some help
in different ways. But we try to keep to the schedule, and,
what's more, we usually succeed!

Each of the groups meet with its teacher approximately twice
a month. This is a chance for the parents and the teacher to
talk about routines and procedures in the classroom, discuss
problems that may have arisen, and work together toward
improving and strengthening the operation of the classroom.

Later in this handbook you will find sections
dealing specifically with what you can do as
a teacher-assistant in the classroom.

In the Family Room:

The Family Room is the place where ideas are shared, plans
blossom, and lots of coffee is consumed. Ann Joyner, program
coordinator of Playgroup, reminds parents that after you have
brought your youngster to his classroom, you are expected to
come to the Family Room.

First, as always, the Family Room will be a place where mothers
can relax (away from the children) and enjoy a coffee break in
the company of friends.

But participation in the Family Room means more than a good cup of coffee and a place to chat and knit. As always when mothers get together, they will want to have this a place for lively discussion and debate on issues that concern us as mothers and as members of this community.

It will be the scene of planned meetings on a variety of topics. Aline Auerbach and Ann Joyner will be having regular discussion meetings in which we have a chance to talk about some of the problems we mothers face in helping our children to grow up.

Other meetings will be set up around questions that <u>you</u> raise. Keep coming to the staff with ideas and suggestions for things that mothers want to know more about—whether it's job opportunities in the neighborhood, facilities for health care, or educational matters like whether or not we should try to teach our pre-schoolers to read. Meetings will then be set up, bringing in outside "experts" to share their information with us where this is needed.

Finally, the Family Room is the place where plans are made and carried out—plans for family outings and trips, for special events like portion suppers and Christmas parties, for fund-raising events like movie showings and bazaars.

In other words, the program in the Family Room can be as exciting and interesting as we can made it <u>together</u>.

<u>Working</u> <u>on</u> <u>Committees</u>:

Committees are what keep the program moving ahead. A number of committees will be set up, and it is hoped that every parent will participate on at least one. (Meetings usually take place in the morning in the Family Room.)

The Committees include:

1. Group Chairmen

   Two mothers from each group might share this job's three responsibilities: (1) setting up the schedule for the parents assisting in the classroom, (2) helping to find temporary escorts for children in the group whose mothers are unable to bring them to Playgroup, and (3) letting the mothers in the group know when their help might be needed on a specific Playgroup project, such as a party or fund-raising event.

2. Equipment Committee

This committee is responsible for the repair and upkeep of Playgroup's equipment, and also makes recommendations for the purchase of new equipment. Mothers with handy (and willing) husbands are particularly urged to join this committee.

3. Newsletter Committee

Two or three parents are needed to put out a monthly newsletter, including items of interest to Playgroup parents and the community.

4. Fund-Raising Committee

Bloomingdale is _always_ "in the red." Fund-raising events— film festivals, bazaars, cake sales—make it possible to provide materials and equipment for the children, and a more varied program for everyone. Bloomingdale has several "tried and true" fund-raising events. We also need new ideas. This committee is vital to the continuation of the program.

5. Schools and Community Affairs

Playgroup parents who are already involved in local school and community affairs (or who want to be) are urged to join this committee. Their job will be to keep abreast of what's going on in the neighborhood and share this information with all of us at Playgroup. They may also be called upon to represent Bloomingdale at school and community meetings.

6. Family Room Committee

We need a group of mothers to act as Family Room "hostesses," to make new mothers feel welcome and comfortable at the program, to scout out ideas and suggestions for Family Room activities, and to help the staff put these suggestions into operation.

7. Secretarial Committee

Can you type? Cut stencils? Run the mimeograph machine? Address envelopes? Playgroup has no secretary this year, and we will need lots of help in putting out the newsletter, typing up proposals to foundations and government (asking for funds), and keeping the office as organized and efficient as possible.

A list of these committees is given out at registration. Please check the committees you are most interested in.

4. PRACTICAL HINTS FOR CLASSROOM ASSISTANTS

What does the teacher expect, when she asks a mother to assist in the classroom?

Mothers who assist there help the teacher to create a friendly and easy atmosphere in which the children can play together, use play materials creatively, and get to know one another. The mothers take their cues from the teachers, stepping in where necessary at their suggestion.

Some parents may feel more comfortable helping the children in one area or another, and you will soon find the places you enjoy working in the most.

Below are some suggestions drawn up by Susan Feingold for small, physical tasks that need to be done to help the children play safely and happily.

Paint Corner

1. Check to see that (a) paint jars are filled
                     (b) there is a brush for every color
                     (c) there is paper on easel.
2. Help child put on smock.
3. Encourage child to replace each brush in its own color.
4. Encourage child to help clean up spilled paint.
5. Write child's name on completed painting (top left corner).
6. Help child take off smock.
7. Be receptive to having child talk about his painting, but avoid asking questions about content.

Workbench

1. Never leave area!
2. Let no more than two to three children work at the same time.
3. Stop other children from playing very close to workbench.
4. Make sure tools do not leave the immediate area.
5. Help children use tools properly.
6. Try to prevent children from accidentally hurting each other with tools.
7. Encourage children to help you put away tools.

Housekeeping Corner

1. Help children not to get too wet at sink. (Roll up sleeves, encourage wearing of aprons.)
2. Try to prevent playdough from becoming water-logged, getting

stuffed into coffee pot spouts or other very unsuitable
places, or being taken to other play areas.
3. Help children take turns washing and drying dishes, playing
   with favorite dolls, etc.
4. Be ready to help and encourage children with dress—up,
   hair—dos, etc.

Water Play

1. Encourage children to wear aprons and roll up sleeves.
2. Supervise pouring of soap flakes and adding of vegetable
   coloring.
3. Prevent children from carrying water into other play areas.
4. Encourage children to exchange water toys.
5. Encourage children to help you mop up.

Block Corner

1. Do not build for child, but assist when he really needs
   help.
2. Help children be aware of other children building near them
   to avoid accidental "toppling."
3. Help children respect each other's work. (I won't let Johnny
   pull down your building, but I won't let you pull down
   Johnny's building either.)
4. See that children help put away blocks so that each kind of
   block is visible and in its own category.

5. GENERAL GUIDELINES FOR WORKING WITH THE CHILDREN

As parents become accustomed to the routines of assisting in
the classroom, they begin to ask how they can focus their
talents and abilities to work more effectively with the young
children and help them in their growth and development in the
classroom. The following suggestions were prepared by Marion
Borenstein:

First, it is of utmost importance for the parent, just as it
is for the teacher, to build a friendly and understanding
relationship with all the children in the classroom. Learn to
accept the child as he or she is, so that the child may in turn
accept you as a responsive person.

Be sure that the child understands what you are saying when
you speak. Try to gain his attention first, and make certain
that your words are clear and simple. If possible, give only one
direction at a time to a child. Be ready to show the child the
meaning of your idea if he does not grasp it readily.

Try to be reasonable and timely from the child's own point of view. Young children can become confused or irritated when rushed or pressured, so do not try to suggest a change of activity without telling him ahead of time. Do not expect him to stop what he is doing at once, but let children finish an activity if at all possible.

If a child refuses your direction, "I don't want to," let a moment go by. Often he will comply if the point is not belabored or argued about. Seek the help of the teacher if you are having difficulty in dealing with a child.

Remember these key points: (They will take on added meaning as you gain more experience and confidence in working with children in the classroom.)

1. Limit directions to essentials.

2. Let the child take responsibility for himself as soon as he is able.

3. Expect children to spill milk or juice, drop puzzles, etc. You can encourage children to help clean up after an accident. Help them learn by experience, but step in to avoid failure and discouragement. Encourage the child to find out and experiment for himself.

4. Expect children to make errors in judgment in taking on new activities.

5. Try to be gentle in manner and tone.

6. Try to avoid holding children to a uniform standard of performance. Never compare him to someone else; praise him for his own achievement.

7. Praise a child when he makes a new step forward. Praise him when he accomplishes something important to him, no matter how insignificant it may appear to you.

8. Give the child a choice of action where this is reasonable, but limit the choice to perhaps one of two choices. For example, "Where would you like to leave your tricycle, John? By the gate or near the door?" Giving children too many choices may be too much for them to handle.

9. If you really cannot allow the child to make the choice—and some situations may call for you to make the decision—be direct and quietly firm with the child: "June, please park the tricycle near the gate and put on your jacket."

10. Avoid nagging; as much as possible avoid conflict and
forcing of issues. We hope children will learn to be
pleasantly cooperative rather than feel forced into doing
what they are told.

6. HOW MOTHERS AND TEACHERS FEEL ABOUT WORKING TOGETHER

Diana Bowstead, a Playgroup mother, writes about her experience
in the program:

"As Bloomingdale mothers, we are all encouraged to take a
very real interest in our children's classroom experience. In
fact, we are asked to share it. As Bloomingdale children, ours
have the rare opportunity of seeing us in a different role:
perhaps one still a little inferior to the teacher, but still a
little more than the old, every-day 'mommy.'

"Mothers share the teacher's work; children share each
other's mothers—the break between home and school is eased for
all concerned.

"We help in the classroom approximately twice a month, doing
everything from setting up equipment and cleaning up messes to
coping with the children who are having trouble getting along
in the group. We are certainly qualified for the first part of
the job; all of us have had all too much experience cleaning up
messes at home. We are qualified for the second part of the job
too; our own children have taught us to recognize fear, anger,
or pain behind a blank or sullen expression of the face of a
child who will not talk or in the destructive behavior of a
child who does not know how to ask for help.

"We take something from this job, too: a new view of our
children. They appear quite different as members of a group,
and we come to understand them as increasingly independent and
distinct individuals. Learning to do this, mothers suffer their
own growing pains. Bloomingdale allows us a 'period of
adjustment' during which we proudly watch our children's
accomplishments while we are still present to protect and hover
over them now and then."

And Joan Sandler, a Playgroup teacher, has this to say about
working in the program:

"Parents add a new richness and dimension to the program. Our
parents brought their own individual talents and abilities to

the classroom and were generally eager to do more in the areas
of storytelling, leading games and creative arts and crafts
projects. I truly felt that more of this should have taken
place and want to say that more and more will take place this
year.

"So don't be shy and tell us what areas of the classroom you
feel special about. We promise not to be shy about asking you
to lend a hand.

"I especially want to say on the part of the teachers that we
have found working and getting to know the parents an enriching
experience which makes life here at Bloomingdale very special.
Each parent contributed her own unique qualities and experience
to the program, and this gave the teachers an opportunity for a
better understanding and appreciation of the children, their
parents and our Bloomingdale community."

FAMILY ROOM CALENDAR

MONDAY	TUESDAY	WEDNESDAY	THURSDAY	FRIDAY
Committees	Discussion Series	Special Topics	Preparing Classroom Materials	Free Day
Fill in as scheduled	(By Registration only) 6 weekly sessions	FEB. 28 "Troublesome" Behavior in Children. When is it "Disruptive"? When is it "Healthy"? In whose eyes? What can Parents do? or Bloomingdale?	FEB. 29	MARCH 1
	MARCH 5 Meeting #1	6 What is happening in our Community? Recent Developments in School Planning, Neighborhood Organizations, etc.	7	8
	MARCH 12 Meeting #2	13 Stretching the Food Budget. How to Eat Well at Low Cost, with Low Calories. Suggested Recipes.	14	15
	MARCH 19 Meeting #3	20 Community Issues and Problems: Reports and Discussion.	21	22
	MARCH 26 Meeting #4	27 Housing: Tenant Problems	28	29

Appendix III

SOME POINTS TO BEAR IN MIND
IN DEVELOPING A DISCUSSION

1. FINDING AN AREA FOR DISCUSSION
   Defining it, in terms of what there is about it that is of
   concern, from personal experience of one parent, broadened to
   include others in the group. "Checking with the group," sometimes in words to see if it is of interest to all, sometimes
   merely stating that this seems to be saying something they all
   want to talk about—and watching the tone of their response.

2. DEVELOPING THE DISCUSSION
   Having parents elaborate the discussion out of specific
   incidents. Encouraging them to describe what they mean by key
   words that suggest the essence of a situation or their or their
   children's feelings in it or about it. Having a parent give
   some brief report of the nature of an episode, what preceded
   it, whether it was usual or not of long standing, etc., and
   encouraging others to do the same. Attempting to get a
   balanced picture—in time— of what the child did——what the
   parent did——what the child felt——————what the parent felt——
   what other children are doing in similar situations——what
   other parents are doing and feeling. Out of this usually comes
   some sense of normal child development, through characteristic
   stages and crises of growth (the "developmental tasks"), of the
   wide range of individual differences and also where behavior
   seems to be out of bounds. Also of stages in the parents' role
   as children grow, and of the varying needs of parents, both as
   individuals and at different times in the family cycle.
   These trends can be underscored if and when they emerge, or
   given as added interpretations drawn from psychological
   knowledge, — but usually only after parents have gone as far
   with it as they can, and stated so that the interpretations are
   closely related to what they have already said.

3. PITFALLS TO AVOID, IF POSSIBLE!
   Having one or more members give advice quickly, without having
   had the group go into a matter; one needs to understand it
   first, and only then can one decide what to do.
   Having one or two members take over the bulk of the talk; this
   calls for encouraging others to react to their comments and

contributions and add their own. Having the group push the
leader for her personal opinion or advice or "what did you do?"
If leader does say what she did, it should be identified as her
personal way of meeting something which may not be right for
others. It is better, however, to avoid this by saying that
each one must decide himself, on the basis of his own understanding of the situation. This the leader will try to help the
group gain, by sharing with other parents, listening to them,
adding ideas that are generally accepted and then leaving
it to the parents to take out of this what seems to fit their
child, their family, their community.

4. This last point, what a parent decides to do, is in a sense the
   end goal of such discussions. Parents should be left to come to
   this in their own due time, and not pressed to announce a
   decision, which may be only half formulated during the discussion and which they should not feel commited to carry through
   if they have reason to change their minds. Hopefully such
   discussions will shake them loose from some of their ways of
   behaving, if they do not seem valid, shift their attitudes and
   expectations where they seem inappropriate, and open the way
   for them to try new ways where they are indicated, and to
   choose those that seem best. This step, sometimes described as
   The Coping Phase, usually comes late but must not be overlooked. Sometimes it comes out of parents' reports of what they
   did between meetings—and how it worked!

[Note: For further discussion of these and other aspects of leadership, see Aline B.
Auerbach, *Parents Learn Through Discussion: Principles and Practises of Parent
Group Discussion.* John Wiley and Sons, 1968.]

Appendix IV

NEWSLETTER
February 16, 1967

PORTION SUPPER SNOWED OUT—NEW DATE SET FOR TUESDAY, FEB. 21

The Blizzard of '67 forced us to postpone our International Portion Supper earlier this month. If you stowed your delectable dish in the freezer, remember to thaw it out in time for the new date:

Tuesday, Feb. 21....5:30 to 7:30 P.M.

at Frederick Douglass Community Center
885 Columbus Avenue
Main Auditorium

Please Remember...If you originally signed up to cook something or help out at the Feb. 8th supper, we're still counting on your help for the 21st. Please contact Playgroup (666-2956) or the office (865-7300) if you have any questions.

Hope the weather man is good to us this time. But unless we have a hurricane or a tornado, we're going ahead with our plans.

FAMILY ROOM DISCUSSION MEETINGS TO BEGIN NEXT WEEK

Parent program director Aline Auerbach, and Mary Eccles, our program coordinator, are starting a series of regular discussion meetings for Playgroup Parents. Two series of meetings—to be held from 10 AM to 11:15 AM in the Family Room—are planned:

(1) If Tuesday is your day at Playgroup, there will be a Tuesday series of every-other-week meetings beginning February 21.

(2) If Wednesday is your regular day, there is a Wednesday series of every-other-week meetings beginning March 1.

Group 1 mothers (whose children are in the five-day group at the Community Center) can sign up with Marion Borenstein for either the Tuesday or Wednesday series, and Group 8 mothers (Friday toddlers) can tell Mary Eccles which day they would like to come.

These discussions will be an opportunity to talk about matters that relate to our children here at Playgroup, at home or in the community. Some of the questions that will probably come up are nightmares, thumb sucking, how your child feels about your leaving him, what the children are getting from nursery school, changes in the children's development, and many others.

Such questions have already been raised in the family room, in the classroom, and in parent–teacher meetings, but this will be your chance to go into them more fully, to bring up what is on your mind and share your ideas and experiences with the other mothers, with the help of Mrs. Auerbach and Mary.

Note: These discussion meetings are different from the regular class parent–teacher meetings, which will be rescheduled. Watch your bulletin board for the new dates.

MEDICAID INFORMATION AND APPLICATIONS AVAILABLE AT PLAYGROUP

A number of Playgroup mothers braved the snow on February 9th to meet with the Medicaid Coordinator of H.I.P., Mr. Maurice Curtis. He described the three ways in which families can take advantage of the free services offered under Medicaid:

(1) Using a private doctor who participates in the Medicaid program. (A list of participating doctors will be published this Spring.)

(2) Using hospital out–patient facilities.

(3) Joining an H.I.P. center, which offers a family physician plus a group of medical specialists.

Mary Eccles has Medicaid application forms which she can help you fill out. Please check with Mary if you have any questions about your eligibility for Medicaid, the services they offer, and how to apply.

HOLIDAYS COMING UP

As a general rule, Playgroup is closed any time the public schools are closed. Here's a reminder of upcoming holiday dates:

February 22.......George Washington's Birthday
March 24 thru 31..Easter. School resumes on April 3.

NEWSLETTER
March 17, 1967

HAPPY (SNOWY) EASTER!

Easter vacation for Playgroup, like the Public Schools, begins on Friday, March 24th. Parties are being planned in the different groups during the week of the 20th. Thursday, March 23rd, will be the last day of school—and we'll see you back again at Playgroup when school resumes on Monday, April 3. Happy Holiday!

Note to mothers whose children don't like eggs: If you'll tint a batch of hard-boiled eggs with Easter Egg colors available in the supermarket, your kids will look forward to peeling and eating the colorful eggs every morning during Easter week.

MORE PARENT DISCUSSION MEETINGS COMING UP: POST-HOLIDAY SCHEDULE

In order that the Easter holiday won't create too big a gap between our parent discussion meetings with Mrs. Auerbach and Mary, we've changed the schedule around slightly:

The Tuesday group resumes after the holiday on April 4th and will meet regularly every other week thereafter.

The Wednesday group will meet two weeks in a row, to make up for the day lost during the holiday. Their meetings will take place on:

      April 5th, April 12th, and then every other week thereafter.

These meetings have been very exciting and very popular...so please try to come to Playgroup early on meeting days so that we can get started on time and make the most of the morning.

LEARN TO SEW...LEARN TO WEAVE

Beginning right after the holiday, Adina Jones is going to be available every Thursday and Friday morning in the Family Room at

the Church to give instruction to interested parents in the fine
art of weaving and in various aspects of sewing, from pinning and
cutting the pattern to the final fitting of the garment. Let Mary
Eccles know if you are interested, so we can plan to get the
materials we need to start us off.

THE MYSTERY OF THE VANISHING MOTHER

Just a reminder that Playgroup cannot run without your help and
cooperation. Mothers, if it's your day to help in the classroom,
please make a special effort to come, and come early. The teachers
must know who they can count on for assistance in the classroom.
They need you, and the children need you.

If it's not your day to help in the classroom, we trust you'll
find your way upstairs to the Family Room and join the rest of the
mothers there. If there is a special reason for you to be away
from the building during the morning, please make sure you check
first with either the teacher or Mary Eccles to tell them where
you'll be.

Remember...The playgroup at the Church is not a licensed
program. This means that you—not the school—must be responsible
for your child and that we must know where you are while your
child is with his group in the program.

PLAYGROUP PARENTS MET ON MARCH 13

Every Playgroup neeting seems to bring a snowstorm, but 28
parents (including three mothers who hope to be in the program
next year) trekked through the slush to 868 Amsterdam Avenue last
Monday evening. We talked about the summer programs—and particularly the difficulty of getting funds to run the programs. It
looks as if funds will be very tight this summer and we will have
to patch together our programs in Riverside and Central Parks out
of whatever staff we can get from the Parks Department, the Health
Department, the Board of Education and the Neighborhood Youth
Corps. But come what may, there WILL BE a program in both parks.

Two committees—fund-raising and membership—were formed. The
fund-raising committee will try to find ways of raising the $1,000

Playgroup needs to finish out this school year (see announcement
of Film Festival below), and the membership committee will launch
a drive to get more and wider membership for BNRC throughout the
community to provide a broader base of support for our efforts to
raise funds for the whole program from public and private sources.

A number of fund-raising projects are already in the works, but
if you have any brainstorms, tell them to fund-raising chairman
Lucille Spivak. She needs your help and your best thinking.

SPRING CLEANING IN THE FAMILY ROOM

...or hadn't you noticed. Parents and staff pitched in this week
to clean up, straighten out and organize the Family Room from top
to bottom. It should now be easy to pick up books you may want to
read, get to materials you need in the supply closet, find the
coffee and even locate the phone!

But...if you do take materials out of the closet, please
remember to put them back as you found them, clear off the table,
throw out the used cups and coffee grounds, and set the room up
for the people who'll use it the next day. They'll do the same for
you.

SCHOLARSHIPS FOR MOTHERS DISCUSSED AT WELFARE LEAGUE MEETING

Mothers from Playgroup and the community met earlier this month
at 868 Amsterdam Avenue with Frances Julty, city-wide coordinator
of Welfare Clients Groups, and learned about a number of training
and scholarship programs available for mothers who want to
complete or continue their education. To learn more about this,
contact Mary Eccles.

Mrs. Julty stressed the benefits to families on welfare who join
local welfare recipients groups. In our neighborhood, the United
Welfare League is affiliated with Mrs. Julty's group, and is
located at 929 Columbus Avenue, near 105th Street. (Phone:
799-6205) The office is open from 9 to 5 weekdays, and is staffed
with people to give help and information as needed.

MEDICAID APPLICATIONS STILL AVAILABLE

Applications for complete, free medical care under the Medicaid Plan are available at Playgroup. Ask Mary Eccles or Bea Schultz for information about who is eligible, the services they offer, and how to apply.

TWO ALL-DAY CONFERENCES OF SPECIAL INTEREST COMING UP IN APRIL

An open invitation has been extended to the West Side Community Conference on "Health Care in the Cities" on Saturday, April 1 at Barnard Hall, Broadway near 116th Street. Morning and afternoon panels will feature speakers on such vital issues as Health Care, Mental Health, Noise and Air Pollution, Hospital Care, Medicare and Medicaid. The program is free, and Mary Eccles can give you the schedule of the various panels and speakers.

On Sunday, April 2 there will be an all-day conference on "Our City's Schools: Problems and Promise" at the Stephen Wise Free Synagogue, 30 West 68th Street. There is a $1 fee for registration and $1 for the luncheon at which Superintendent of Schools Donovan will be the speaker. Talk to Mary Eccles about the schedule of workshops if you are interested.

MAKE PLANS NOW FOR SUMMER CAMP PROGRAMS

The Children's Aid Society (Douglass Community Center at 885 Columbus Avenue) has three camp programs for youngsters this summer:

Camp (sleep-away)...3 week sessions for boys and girls 8 to 12, $42.

Day Camp (on Staten Island)...for boys and girls 8 to 11, $5 per week includes bus transportation.

Home Camp (at the Community Center)...boys and girls 6 and 6. $5 per week, for a full day, 9 AM to 5 PM program.

DECEMBER NEWSLETTER 1967

THE CHRISTMAS BAZAAR NEEDS YOU

Lots of extra hands will be needed to get the Bazaar going. Our supplies of things to sell are good, but we need mothers to get the room set up and do the selling.

Setting up will take place on Wed. & Thurs., Dec. 13 & 14.

We open for business on Friday the 15th and the Bazaar continues through Saturday the 16th, both days from 10 AM until 6 PM.

Let Bazaar Chairman Nina Feldman know which days or hours she can count on you to set up or sell.

 ### DON'T be LATE in '68!

Playgroup begins at 9:15 AM. When you don't arrive till 10, it means that your child has missed one-third of his entire school day!

It also means he misses activities, fun and instruction, and his late arrival interrupts what the other children are working at.

Coming to school on time—the morning routine of taking off his coat with the other children and being greeted by teacher and classmates—is a very real part of your child's school experience. Don't be late in '68!

We want your ideas for what

XMAS VACATION

DEC. 25 – JAN. 1

SCHOOL STARTS JAN. 2

1968

AFTER THE BAZAAR?

will happen in the Family Room after the Bazaar is over. Mothers and staff have already been talking about this, and here are some of their ideas:

More regular discussions on what's going on in the community and city...school and decentralization affairs... local anti-poverty projects... job and training opportunities ...political and current events.

"Classes" in sewing and other handwork...grooming and make-up sessions. Our mothers have lots of talent, and can share their skills with those who want to learn.

Special morning meetings on health matters, such as immunizations and preventive medicine, and family planning.

What do you want to do in the Family Room? Come in and speak up—and you'll find that your ideas are listened to!

Dear Bloomingdale Parent,

You are Cordially Invited

to attend

A Supper Meeting

To discuss recent developments

Toward the Decentralization of the Public Schools

and what this will mean

to families in our community.

Place: Playgroup
         240 West 102nd Street

Date: Thursday, January 25th, 1968

Time: 6 PM...supper.
         7 PM...meeting will begin.

Discussion Chairman: Mrs. Aline B. Auerbach, who has had
         an opportunity to discuss decentralization with
         educators, administrators and parents in many
         parts of the city.

The Children are invited to come along too.
They will be supervised while the meeting is under way.

Supper will be a simple spaghetti and salad affair, served
buffet style.

If you make a great spaghetti sauce or good cookies or
brownies for dessert, bring some along with you to add to the
buffet.

There will be a list posted at Playgroup to sign up for the
meeting. Please add your name to this list if you plan to attend,
so that we can know how many places to set for supper.

Bloomingdale parents...

You are cordially invited
urgently needed
and
desperately wanted

at a big

'WORK-IN'

Monday, February 19, 1968
at Playgroup - 240 W. 102nd
from 7 p.m. on ...

To — repair equipment
paint furniture
organize books and materials
set up our new storage room

Bring children
if necessary

Bring husbands
if they will work!

SMALL PARENT DISCUSSION GROUP:
Six weekly meetings on Tuesdays at 10 AM Beginning March 5th, 1968

These meetings will take up the main problems parents have on their minds about their children at home, in playgroup and school and in the neighborhood—and even in the larger world, if the parents wish this. The discussions will be led by Mrs. Auerbach and will be directed toward what children really need and what parents can do to help them.

The meetings will be in a _quiet_ room, so that parents can really listen to one another and hear themselves think.

The group will be limited to fifteen mothers who want to attend regularly each week, registered in order of their application. It is open to mothers whose children are in any of the different playgroups. Arrangements will be made for children who are not in the playgroups that day.

If you wish to join this group, please sign below and give the slip to Bea Schutz or Dorothy Harrison.

I would like to join the parent discussion group to be held Tuesdays at 10 AM, for six weekly sessions beginning March 5th.

Signed _____

date _____

Estimada Señora

Ud está cordialmente invitada
Para asistir a la reunión café
Que sean Bienveni dos las nuevas madres
Al Programa Familiar Bloomingdale.

recuerde
ese día ↗

Miercoles, Noviembre 15
a los 10 A.M.
868 Amsterdam Avenue

Si el miércoles no es el día que tu
hijo asiste al grupo de juego, traélo
contigo al family room. Qué abrá
sorpresas y los niños pasarán un rato
agradable.

Por favor trate de venir.

Sinceramente,

Ann Joyner

Note: This flyer, like
all notices, was
sent out in both
Spanish and English
to all families.

BLOOMINGDALE BUSYNESS

NOVEMBER, 1970

Bloomingdale Family Program—Operation Head Start
240 West 102 Street—663-4067,8

FAMILY ROOM PROGRAM

The Family Room is YOURS.
Please suggest to Sonia ideas
for what you'd like to do. We
hope to have both Spanish and
English lessons, and perhaps a
High School equivalency program. Let's have more ideas
soon!

DOCTORS and DENTISTS

Safeguarding our children's
health is part of the Bloomingdale Head Start program.
Medical and dental exams can
be arranged through Lucy
Sharpe. We must have a record
of the children's immunizations. This year shots against
German Measles are required. A
doctor will come to the school
to give them, without charge.
Also, the children will all
have their eyes examined, also
at the school and without
charge.

IN THE KITCHEN

All of our children are
served a well-balanced lunch
each day, as well as juice and
cookies. We try to make the
food as interesting and varied
as possible. We have a menu
committee to help plan the
meals. If you'd like to be on
this committee, or if you have
ideas or recipes you'd like to
see used, Joyce and Annamarie
are waiting to hear from you.

PROGRAMA DEL SALON DE LA FAMILIA

El Salón de la Familia está
a sus órdenes; por favor
sugiera algunas ideas que
usted crea convenientes.
Esperamos tener lecciones en
español y en inglés, y quizás
programas de equivalencia de
Escuela Superior. Sugiéranos
nuevas ideas pronto!

DOCTORES y DENTISTAS

El cuido de la salud de los
niños es parte del programa
Head Start Bloomingdale.
Exámenes físicos y dentales se
pueden arreglar con Lucy
Sharpe. Tenemos que tener el
record de inmunización de los
niños. Las inyecciones de este
año contra sarampión alemán
el son necesarias.

Un doctor vendrá a la
escuela a ponerlas
gratuitamente.

EN LA COCINA

A todos nuestros niños se
les sirve un almuerzo bien
balanceado cada día, así como
galleticas y jugos. Tratamos
de hacer el alimento lo más
interesante y variado posible.

Tenemos un comité que nos
ayuda a preparar el menú de
las comidas. Si usted quiere
estar en esta junta, o si
usted tiene ideas o recetas

If you'd like to bake goodies at home for the children's dessert, you can use the school's supplies of flour, etc. See Joyce or Annamarie for more information.

Two absolutely delicious meals have already been cooked by our parents.

CAN YOU HELP???????

We need people who can take care of children whose mothers have been taken to the hospital for emergency care. You will be paid for caring for children, in your home, until the mother is better. If you can help, see Sonia or Susan.

BE SURE TO NOTE————

The large Bulletin Board to your right as you enter the school. It holds news of school and community events, available jobs, health services, etc. There is also a Bulletin Board in the Family Room, and notices of meetings, etc. are posted on the front doors of the school and the classrooms. Watch for them all.

que le gustaría que se usaran, Joyce y Annamarie esperan que usted se comunique con ellas.

Si a usted le gusta hornear golosinas en su casa para postres de los niños, puede usar los abastecimientos de harina de la escuela. Véa a Joyce y Annamarie para más información.

Dos comidas absolutamente deliciosas han sido ya preparadas por los padres.

PUEDE USTED AYUDAR?????

Se necesitan madres que puedan hacerse cargo de niños, cuando las madres sean hospitalizadas en caso de emergencia. Se les pagará por el cuido de los niños. El cuido será en la casa de las encargadas. Si puede ayudar, comuníquese con Susan o Sonia. Gracias.

SCHOOL CLOSED—ESCUELA CERRADA

Thanksgiving —Thurs, Nov. 26
           & Fri., Nov. 27.
           Jueves 26 de nov. y
           viernes 27 de nov.

Christmas   —Navidad—Thurs.,
           Dec. 24 through Fri,
           Jan. 1. Jueves 24 de
           diciembre a viernes
           1 de enero.

Martin Luther King's Birthday
           Fri., Jan. 15.
           Viernes 15 de enero.

HELP!!!!!!!!!!

Despite our Head Start funding, Bloomingdale still needs money! We must raise an additional $16,000. We can all help in many ways. For example:

If you have had experience in writing funding proposals to foundations, please see Susan.

Join the Fund-raising Committee. If you have any ideas for ways we can make money, leave a note for chairman Mrs. Consuela Morel in the Family Room.

Buy our Christmas Cards. They'll soon be on sale for 50¢ for a box of 10. They're most attractive and are suitable for notes all year long.

WATCH FOR A GALA FUND-RAISING DANCE TO BE HELD EARLY NEXT YEAR!!!

Bring in old clothes and furniture, craft materials for your children's class, a treat for the children. All such contributions count towards the matching funds we must provide to Head Start. So does the time you spend helping in your child's class, or participating in Family Room activities. Be sure to tell Sonia what you bring in and how much time you spend at the school.

SUGGESTIONS FOR THINGS PARENTS CAN BRING IN TO BE USED IN CLASS

1—Empty spools.
2—String, yarn, fabric for collages.
3—Telephone wire.
4—Meat trays.
5—Dress-up clothes (skirts, dresses, men's & ladies' shoes, jewelry, etc.)
6—Plastic squeeze bottles.
7—Rollers from paper towels and toilet paper.
8—Newspaper.
9—Metal gadgets.
10—Noodles, macaroni.
11—Anything else that you think would enrich the program.

BLOOMINGDALE BUSYNESS: Issued by the Bloomingdale Family Program, Operation Head Start, 240 W. 102 Street.

Editor: Eda Krantz
Translation: Sonia Lidell, Phyllis Sneed.

Suggestions and contributions to this newsletter are eagerly welcomed. Just leave notes for me with Sonia in the Family Room.

Eda Krantz

WHEN YOU'RE IN CLASS——

Parent participation in the classroom is an important part of the Bloomingdale program. Below are some suggestions for when it's your turn to help.

ART CORNER:

See that the child has
adequate supplies for his
project.

Painting:
1—See that child has one
   brush for each paint.
2—Each child should have a
   smock.
3—Put clean paper on easel.
4—Put child's name in upper
   left hand corner of
   painting.

Collage:

1—See that child has
   adequate paste and try to
   help him use it sparingly.
2—See that child has a good
   supply of materials to be
   pasted.
3—See that children wash
   their hands when through,
   then remove smock before
   leaving area.
If you enjoy doing these
activities, and finger
painting, manipulating clay,
etc., it helps the
children to enjoy them too.

HOUSKEEPING AREA:

1—Be ready to enter into
   imaginative play. Ask
   child to make coffee for
   you or other children, for
   example.
2—Help with dress up or
   hair-do.

3—Try to keep play—dough in
   housekeeping area.
4—Help children take turns
   with dolls and other
   housekeeping toys.

BLOCK AREA:

1—Do not build for child,
   but be prepared to help
   him when he needs it.
   Sometimes (especially with
   3's) it helps to begin to
   build yourself.
2—Help children to put
   blocks away according to
   size and shape, so each
   shape is visible.
3—Help children to respect
   each other's work. Say,
   "I won't let Johnny push
   your tower, but I can't
   let you push his down
   either."

REQUESTS TO PARENTS

Please, please, please get
your child to school on time,
so he can get the full
benefits of the program. The
morning session begins at 9:00
a.m., the afternoon session at
12:45.

Afternoon parents—please
don't give your child lunch
at home, or let him fill up on
snacks. Eating lunch together
is an important part of the
program, that we'd like all of
the children to share!

Appendix V

BY-LAWS——BLOOMINGDALE FAMILY PROGRAM

ARTICLE I—Affiliation

The Bloomingdale Family Program is a subsidiary of the Bloomingdale Neighborhood Conservation Association, Inc.

ARTICLE II—Office

The Family Program shall maintain an office within the Borough of Manhattan, New York, New York, at a place to be determined by the Steering Committee.

ARTICLE III—Purpose

The purpose of the Family Program is to conduct programs for children, for parents, and for the members of the community, which programs shall be directed toward the educational and mental health of children.

ARTICLE IV—Membership

Membership shall be available to any person, firm, or corporation that pays $1.00 dues annually or pays $1.00 or more of tuition annually toward a program of the Family Program or contributes $1.00 or more annually. A membership application shall be filled out by such person, firm, or corporation, evidencing a desire to be a member.

ARTICLE V—Meetings

1. Annual Meeting. The annual meeting of the members, at which elections shall be conducted, shall be held in the spring of each year at a time and place to be determined by the Steering Committee. Ten days written notice of such meeting shall be given all the members.

2. Steering Committee meetings shall be held at least once every two months at times and places to be determined in advance by the Executive Committee. Five days written notice shall be given to Steering Committee members.

3. Executive Committee meetings shall be held at least once each month at a time and place to be determined by the Executive Committee at the commencement of the year.

4. There shall be at least two membership meetings each year. The annual meeting shall constitute one of said two meetings.

The other membership meeting shall take place in the fall at a time and place to be determined by the Steering Committee. Three days written notice shall be given to all members.

5. Special meetings of the members may be called at any time by the Executive Committee; special meetings shall be called by the Executive Committee at the request of 15 members. Five days written notice shall be given of all such meetings.

6. A special meeting of the Executive Committee shall be called by the Chairman at the request of two members of the Executive Committee on three days written notice, or at the Chairman's discretion.

7. A special meeting of the Steering Committee shall be called by the Chairman at the request of one-fourth of the members of the Steering Committee or seven members of the Steering Committee, whichever is fewer. Three days written or oral notice of such meetings shall be given.

8. All notices as specified above shall state the time, place and purpose of the meeting. Any notices contained in news-letters or other general mailings shall constitute due notice as specified above.

9. One-fifth of the members of the Family Program, or 25 members, whichever is fewer, shall constitute a quorum for the transaction of business at any general membership meeting. Except on ratifying amendment to these by-laws, a majority of those present and voting shall prevail.

ARTICLE VI—Officers

1. The officers of the Family Program shall be parents currently participating in a program of the Family Program at the time of their election and shall remain participating parents to maintain their positions. They shall not be staff members.

2. The officers of the Family Program shall consist of the Chairman, the Vice-Chairman, the recording secretary, the corresponding secretary, the financial secretary, and the two members-at-large of the Executive Committee. Together they shall comprise the Executive Committee.

3. The Chairman shall preside over all meetings and shall be the chief executive officer of the Program.

4. The Vice-Chairman shall perform the duties of the Chairman in the absence of the Chairman; shall be responsible for the functioning of the committee structure.

5. The recording secretary shall take, prepare, and keep for reference minutes of all meetings of the Executive Committee, Steering Committee, and general membership; and shall read such minutes at all meetings specified above.

6. The corresponding secretary shall be responsible for notifying members of all meetings; and shall coordinate the secretarial functions of the Program.

7. The financial secretary shall prepare the budget; and shall present current financial reports at all meetings of the Steering Committee and general membership.

8. Checks shall be co-signed by the chairman of the Bloomingdale Neighborhood Conservation Association, Inc., and the Chairman of the Family Program or the financial secretary of the Family Program.

ARTICLE VII—Executive Committee

1. All offices except those of the two members-at-large shall be filled by nomination from the floor at the Spring Annual Meeting. Persons nominated at this time must be parents currently participating in a program of the Family Program or parents of children enrolled in such program for the following school year. Their positions are vacated automatically if the child does not attend, or ceases to attend, such program.

2. The two at-large positions shall be filled by nomination from the floor at the Fall membership meeting. The nominees shall consist only of new parents unless none is willing to serve. They must be parents currently participating in a program of the Family Program at the time of their election and must remain participating parents to retain their positions.

3. The Executive Committee shall be responsible for the day to day operation of the Family Program; shall carry out the policy decisions of the Steering Committee; shall report to the Steering Committee at each meeting of the Steering Committee.

4. If any office excepting that of Chairman becomes vacant, it shall be filled by election at the next meeting of the Steering Committee, and the person elected shall serve until the next general membership meeting. If the chairmanship becomes vacant, the Vice-Chairman shall succeed to the office of Chairman and shall retain such position, subject to the following, until the next Annual Meeting.

5. Any officer may be removed from office by a two-thirds vote

of Executive Committee members or of the members voting at
any meeting called for that purpose. Any officer may be
elected to succeed himself in office.

ARTICLE VIII—Steering Committee

A. The Steering Committee shall consist of the following:

1. All class mothers (group chairmen) as elected by the
   mothers of children in the particular classes. A meeting
   by class of the mothers in each class shall be called by
   the Vice-Chairman sometime in the first month of the
   school year for the purpose of conducting an election. The
   mothers in each class shall decide whether to elect a
   class mother to serve for the entire school year or
   whether the position of class mother should rotate among
   more than one mother in the class. Any class mother whose
   child ceases to be in attendance shall automatically
   vacate her position.

2. One chairman and one co-chairman from each committee. The
   committee chairmen shall be chosen by the respective
   committees in the spring. Persons elected committee chairmen at this time must be parents currently participating
   in a program of the Family Program or parents of children
   enrolled in such program for the following school year.
   Their positions are vacated automatically if the child
   does not attend, or ceases to attend, such program. A
   co-chairman for each committee shall be chosen by the
   respective committees in the fall. These nominees shall
   consist only of new parents, unless none is willing to
   serve.

3. A maximum of 15 supporters of the Bloomingdale Family
   Program from the community at large, who are invited to
   join the Steering Committee by selection of the Executive
   Committee with the approval of the Steering Committee.
   Persons may be invited to join the Steering Committee, up
   to the maximum number of 15, throughout the year. No
   person in this category shall be the parent of a child
   enrolled in any program of the Family Program.

B. No staff member shall serve on the Steering Committee.

C. The Steering Committee may declare that a committee chairmanship or co-chairmanship or class mother position is vacant.
   The Vice-Chairman will call a meeting of the affected
   committee or class for the purpose of holding a new election.

D. The Steering Committee shall be responsible for formulating policy for and guiding the direction of the Family Program and its subsidiary programs.

ARTICLE IX—Recall

Notice of all decisions of the Steering Committee and any implementation by the Executive Committee shall be furnished to the membership within three days by notice posted in the family room. Fifteen members may petition for a special membership meeting at which the membership shall vote on whether to override said decision(s). Majority vote of those present shall prevail. Said meeting must be called by the Chairman within ten days of the filing of the petition, and written notice of the meeting and agenda shall be mailed at least four days prior to the meeting.

ARTICLE X—Staff

1. All applicants for the position of Education or other Director shall be interviewed by a special committee of the Steering Committee set up for this purpose. The Steering Committee's decision is subject to the approval of the membership. Any Director must sign a contract before hire.

2. The Education Director shall hire and supervise the staff, subject to budget limitations and subject to other requirements as to number, salary, and contractual requirements, as determined in advance by the Steering Committee.

ARTICLE XI—Committee Structure

1. The number and functions of the standing committees shall be determined in advance by the Steering Committee.

2. All committees may adopt their own by-laws subject to the approval of the Steering Committee.

3. The Vice-Chairman and the recording secretary shall constitute a standing by-law committee. They shall be responsible for keeping the by-laws up to date and recommending changes or additions to the by-laws to the general membership.

ARTICLES XII—Miscellaneous

1. In the event that a husband and wife are both members, together they shall have but one full vote, which either may exercise.

2. All meetings shall be conducted in accordance with Roberts' Rules of Order, unless otherwise specified herein.

3. A vote of two-thirds of the members present and voting at a regular membership meeting or special meeting called for this purpose shall ratify these by-laws.

4. Two-thirds of the members present and voting at a membership meeting shall be necessary to amend these by-laws.

5. All elections shall be by secret ballot.

[Note: These by-laws have recently been amended. The Steering Committee has been eliminated to provide a structure that is in keeping with the Head Start program.]

Appendix VI

A PROPOSAL TO DEVELOP "IN-BUILDING" PARENT-CHILD CENTERS
AS SATELLITES OF THE BLOOMINGDALE FAMILY PROGRAM.

Bloomingdale Family Program
868 Amsterdam Avenue
New York, N.Y. 10025

Background

The Bloomingdale Family Program, since its inception in 1960,
has created educational and recreational programs for parents and
children in the Bloomingdale community (96th to 110th Streets on
the West Side of Manhattan). The programs began as part of a
neighborhood Conservation Project, a joint City and private effort
to preserve and upgrade housing and other neighborhood conditions
in this multi-racial area just south of Harlem. As parents became
more involved in the Family Program, they increasingly assumed
responsibility for its control and direction. Since January 1966
the Family Program has been governed by its own Board of
Directors, a completely independent body on which neighborhood
families (primarily low-income) have the majority representation.

During the past eight years, the program has worked with a wide
range of families. Always an integrated program, it reflects the
mixed character of the neighborhood, which includes not only
Negro, Puerto Rican, Oriental and white residents of varying
income levels, but also large numbers of new immigrants from
Haiti, Cuba and the Dominican Republic.

The program presently offers free playgroups for children two to
five years old. Inaugurated several years in advance of Head
Start, these playgroups provided a model for Head Start's present
emphasis on parent participation. Bloomingdale parents participate
fully in the operation and direction of the program, both in and
out of the classrooms. Bloomingdale's work in this area has been
strengthened by a three-year demonstration grant from the Fund
for the Advancement of Education of the Ford Foundation, to
develop new approaches to reaching parents and involving them in
their children's learning. This demonstration project, now in its
final year, is currently under the direction of Mrs. Aline B.
Auerbach, formerly assistant director of the Child Study Association of America.

During the summers, Bloomingdale coordinates large community
recreation programs in Riverside Park (103rd Street) and Central
Park (106th Street). Hundreds of people of all ages use the pro-

grams every day. The significance and popularity of these programs
lie in the fact that, unlike programs which are available on a
piecemeal basis to individual family members, the park programs
offer the only setting in which an entire family can participate
all summer long as a unit.

Largely through the summer programs, Bloomingdale has come to
know many of the very poorest families in the community. The
winter playgroups and even Head Start—our own and others—have
tended to serve the upward aspiring families, but have not always
been successful in involving a significant number of families from
the worst blocks in the neighborhood. In the main, these programs
have not been relevant to the lives of those living on the
deteriorated, densely overcrowded tenement blocks forming a large
part of the Bloomingdale neighborhood and characteristic of urban
slum and ghetto areas through this and other cities.

Rationale of the In-Building Project

The proposed In-Building project is conceived as an extension of
the Family Program, offering concrete service to parents and
children through small centers located within the buildings on the
immediate slum blocks of the Bloomingdale neighborhood. This is a
poverty pocket once designated for massive demolition, but now
literally abandoned by the city and the private landlords as urban
renewal has focused on other areas.

Participation in the Family Program has always been a significant experience for most of the parents, including those from the
poorest blocks. We know there is real strength in the program when
we see these parents regularly take their place among the leadership of local school-parent groups, community action programs,
welfare recipients leagues and other groups seeking solutions to
the problems of the neighborhood. The difficulty has been that not
enough of the very poor have been motivated or able to participate
in the Family Program in its present shape. We have made a continuing effort to draw them into the program, but have generally
been successful only when arrangements were made for other parents
to "escort" their children to and from the playgroups on a regular
basis.

There are many and complex reasons why these parents have not
entered into the community services that are available to them.
Large families, overcrowded living space, urgent concerns about
day-to-day subsistance, one-parent homes, inadequate clothing,
poor health, isolation—these tell only part of the story. These
problems are complicated by a floating population of men, whose

presence cannot be officially acknowledged to the Welfare Department or census takers, but who present a situation which deeply
affects the mothers and children. Surrounding the families on
these blocks is the constant impact of drug addiction, prostitu-
tion, and alcoholism, compounded by constant unemployment.

It is our intention in the In-Building project to explore new
patterns of participation for these families in a program that is
flexible and responsive to their particular needs and the means by
which they manage to survive under impossible circumstances.

From our experience with many of these families, we believe
that most parents, no matter how pressed they may be, demonstrate great concern and ingenuity in caring for their children.
While they may see no exit for themselves from the cycle of
poverty, they hope for a better life for their families. These
parents have the potential capacity to make changes in their own
and their children's environments. It is to this capacity for
change and self-help that the In-Building program will address
itself.

Description of the In-Building Centers

Three separate centers will be set up in store fronts or dwell-
ing units in areas of slum housing, and will each serve inten-
sively twenty to thirty families living on the immediate block.
Other individuals from the block will also be served in a less
comprehensive way as they make use of its facilities and staff
around a single problem or situation.

Each center will be large enough to provide flexibility in use,
reflecting the need for different activities at different hours of
the day, and the unique character of the particular blocks served.
Each center will have a Family Room, a Nursery, and at least one
private room for conferences, counselling and interviews, in
addition to a kitchen and at least one bathroom. Office space for
the central coordinating staff will also be provided.

The centers will offer a succession of services through which
the children will move as they mature and which the parents can
use in accordance with their needs:

1. Creche and Nursery, where infants and young children can be
   left on a temporary or emergency basis to permit the parents
   to participate in center activities or to handle pressing
   family needs.

Simple group activities for the children will be begun here, combined with other preschool settings as the children are ready for it (i.e. Bloomingdale playgroups, Head Start, other neighborhood preschool or day care facility).

The Creche and nursery would be supervised by paid parents who would receive continuing inservice training and direction from a skilled Head Teacher.

2. After School Activities, including opportunities both for outdoor play and for quiet homework and study not possible in the typically tiny, overcrowded apartments.

   Neighborhood aides, Neighborhood Youth Corps and Vista workers, and college students would assist in carrying out this phase of the program under appropriate supervision and coordination.

3. The Family Room, where there will be an informal atmosphere for socializing, meetings, discussions and relaxation. Activities here will be determined by the wishes of the parents. Parents and children in the In-Building centers will be considered members of the Family Program, and joint events and activities will be planned throughout the year in an effort to draw these families into a broader community orbit.

4. Health and Mental Health Care, from pre-natal care through adulthood, would be available through the comprehensive family care service of St. Luke's Hospital Community Health Program. Regular visits to the In-Building centers by a public health nurse and consultant pediatrician will re-inforce the utilization of available medical services. In addition, individual and group counselling by the staff social worker will be supplemented by regular contact with mental health consultants.

5. Training Program. For those mothers who would be interested (including teenage girls and other relatives who may already carry much of the responsibility for infant and child care) training programs will be set up in the handling of children in infancy and the early years, geared toward:

   (1) Development of the children's physical, intellectual, emotional and social health and maturation.

   (2) Improving the quality of the mother-child interaction, thus enriching their own parenthood.

   (3) Future further training toward employment in services involving children.

Modest stipends will be paid to parents in return for participating in the training program, or in return for services
rendered in the various aspects of the operation of the
centers.

Research

  Research growing out of the program will be of two kinds,
descriptive and qualitative. (1) A basic description of the
families participating in the centers will be prepared, including
cultural background, family size and make-up, and other pertinent
information. (2) Instruments will be developed to measure changes
that occur, if any, in such areas as participation, child-rearing
styles, relation of participation to children's progress in
school, parental values and interest, and patterns of
communication.

Personnel

  There will be a central coordinating staff for planning, liaison
and administration, consisting of:

  Project Director Administrator: A person with either a social
    work or educational background, with experience in com-
    munity programs or adult education and training programs.
    Responsible for hiring staff, disbursal of all funds.
                                                    (full-time)

  Parent Development and Training Specialist: This role includes
    responsibility for the inservice training of the profes-
    sional and non-professional staff to help them carry out the
    parent-training program and other aspects of the project.
                                                    (part-time)

  Social Worker: to be assisted in the three centers by graduate
    students. The Columbia University School of Social Work is
    very interested in this project, and will provide students
    to work under supervision in the In-Building centers.
                                                    (full-time)

  Head Teacher: To train and supervise the parent aides carrying
    out the nursery program in the three centers.   (part-time)

  Secretary-Bookkeeper: To assist in all aspects of administration
    and record-keeping.   (full-time)

  Research Director: To be assisted by graduate students.
                                                    (part-time)

The staffs for each individual center will include a team of
workers carrying out their various roles under the supervision of
the project director:

Family Room Worker: A professional or trained nonprofessional
    with skills in group work to coordinate activities in the
    Family Room and involve parents in the program.

                           (One full—time per each center)

Teacher Aides: To run the creche and nursery programs in the
    centers.   (One full—time per each center)

Neighborhood and Community Workers: Funds will be provided to
    hire, on part—time or full—time bases, community residents
    to serve in a variety of roles (escort, after—school
    recreation aides, etc.) with appropriate training and
    supervision.

A public health nurse will be on each of the premises at a
specified time each week to supervise the families' health care
and arrange for examinations and treatment. Escorts and/or baby-
sitting will be provided to assist the families in attending to
necessary health care. A consultant pediatrician will be available
on a regular basis. Mental health consultation will be provided
regarding individual problems of children and/or parents and to
work closely with the social worker on plans for clinical evaluation and referral for individual treatment when necessary.

Time Schedule

A three—year pilot study is proposed, with the first four months
of the first year's operation devoted to planning, selection and
orientation of staff, and involving parents in the planning and
recruitment of families to make up the Center population. Budget
figures included here cover only the first year's operation of the
program. The two subsequent years would see a reduction in the
estimated expenditures where capital purchases and non—recurring
costs are involved.

Index